MW01103430

Safe Third Countries

Safe Third Countries
Extending the EU Asylum and Immigration Policies to Central and Eastern Europe

Sandra Lavenex

Central European University Press

Published by
Central European University Press

Október 6. utca 12
H-1051 Budapest
Hungary

400 West 59th Street
New York, NY 10019
USA

Distributed in the UK and Western Europe by
Plymbridge Distributors Ltd.
Estover Road, Plymouth PL6 7PZ
United Kingdom

ISBN 963-9116-44-0 Paperback

Library of Congress Cataloging in Publication Data
A CIP catalog record for this book is available upon request

Cover design by **Picture Elements**

Printed in Hungary by **Akaprint**

To M. I. H.

Contents

Preface

This book analyses the bilateral and multilateral processes by which the countries of Central and Eastern Europe are gradually being incorporated into EU asylum and immigration policies. The extension of the EU refugee regime is on the one hand caused by the external effects of Western European policies, and on the other hand has become an integral part of the EU enlargement process. Highlighting the complex entanglement of domestic policies, European co-operation and international relations, this book analyses these processes from the point of view of their effects on the Central and Eastern European countries, the project of Eastern enlargement and the principles, norms and rules of the international refugee regime.

The book pursues the double goal of presenting a comprehensive introduction to contemporary refugee policy in Europe and of highlighting the dynamics of EU eastward enlargement in this policy field as follows. Chapter 1 presents the issue of refugee policy in an international relations context, focusing on its historical development, main legal provisions, and its normative and institutional foundations. Turning to the European context, Chapter 2 analyses the emergence and evolution of the European refugee regime, and its principal normative and institutional elements. Chapter 3 analyses the extension of EU asylum and immigration policies to the countries of Central and Eastern Europe with special reference to the processes promoting the exportation of this 'acquis' to the CEECs at the intergovernmental level, in the activities of international organisations and NGOs and in the context of the pre-accession strategy of the European Union. Using a country-specific approach, Chapter 4 goes on to explore the way in which the CEECs have adopted the European 'acquis' and adapted to the European asylum and immigration paradigm in an attempt to simultaneously 'join Europe' and to adjust to their transformation from being countries of emigration to countries of immigration. Chapter 5 examines the comprehensive impact of the extension of the European refugee regime on the principles, norms and rules governing international co-operation in this field. Finally, the conclusion recapitulates the findings of the previous chapters against the backdrop of a future eastward enlargement of the EU and the need to accommodate immigration controls with the demands of international human rights norms.

My thanks go to all those who have helped me with the collection of data and who were willing to share their insights into these processes with me. I am particularly grateful to Andrea Lenschow and Dirk Lehmkuhl for their helpful comments on earlier versions of the manuscript, to Heather Grabbe for widening my knowledge on the question of EU enlargement, to the participants of the 1998 European Forum on International Migrations at the European University Institute in Florence for fruitful conversations, to Clare Tame for the enriching editing, to the European University Institute for offering me a splendid working environment, and, finally, to all friends who have supported and encouraged me in this enterprise.

1 Refugees and International Relations

For almost four decades, the movement of persons from and through Central and Eastern Europe to Western Europe was only possible on an exceptional basis. The metaphor of the 'iron curtain' vividly expresses this repression of free movement. Under the Communist regimes, citizens of Central and Eastern Europe were prevented from moving, or even travelling, to the West by an extensive system of exit controls and the military surveillance of the borders to Western Europe.

On the other side of the 'curtain', democratic regimes had long held a liberal stance on migration, rooted in the belief of a citizen's right to choose freely his or her place of residence. Part of this liberal approach was the establishment of an international regime for the protection of refugees within the framework of the United Nations, designed to provide relief for individuals whose basic human rights and fundamental freedoms had been violated in their home country. At the domestic level, these provisions were implemented in asylum laws, and some Western European countries enshrined the right to asylum in their national constitutions. Under the influence of 'cold war' ideology, persons emigrating from Central and Eastern Europe were welcomed by the West as 'fighters for liberty' and were generally admitted as refugees under the asylum scheme.

Today, Western migration regimes have undergone a profound transformation. The opening up of the Eastern bloc in 1989 coincided with the gradual institutionalisation of restrictive asylum and immigration regulations in the European Union. This 'about-turn' in Western European migration policies can be traced back to the economic recession of the mid-1970s, after which all Western European countries revised their approach to economic immigration. In the light of rising numbers of asylum seekers and changes in the causes of forced migration the world over, this restrictive trend also reached the field of asylum policies. Since the mid-1980s, efforts to combat illegal immigration and to reduce the number of asylum seekers have increasingly been co-ordinated at the European level and are now an integral part of European Union (EU) policies.

This book addresses the reshaping of migration regimes between the countries of Central and Eastern Europe, subsequently referred to as CEECs, and Western European countries in the 1990s, placing particular emphasis on refugee policy. The CEECs includes the ten applicants for EU membership: Bulgaria, the Czech Republic, Estonia, Hungary, Latvia, Lithuania, Poland, Romania, Slovakia and Slovenia. The focus on the category of refugees is particularly challenging given the codification of this policy field in an international regime after World War II, as they constitute an exception to the discretionary power of sovereign states to control the entry and residence of aliens on their territory. Under human rights law, refugees are defined as persons who are forced to leave their country of origin because their life or freedom is threatened, and the prohibition against returning such a person to a place where his or her basic human rights are threatened has evolved into a fundamental principle of international law. This is the central difference between the right of asylum as an international institution and immigration policies as a privilege of the state: in the case of asylum seekers and refugees, state sovereignty is circumscribed by the universality of human rights norms.

In a context of increasingly restrictive attitudes on the entry of non-nationals to the West, an examination of this category of forced migrants is likely to highlight key aspects of the relationship between the norm of state sovereignty, implying control over territory and population, the dynamics of European integration, and the protection of universal human rights which apply to all individuals irrespective of nationality. It is in this intricate interplay of international interdependence, human rights, and national sovereignty that the legal concept of territorial asylum has evolved both internationally and domestically in the course of the twentieth century.

The central argument of this book is that Western European states, fearing large-scale immigration from and through Central and Eastern Europe into their territories, have adopted a preventive stance and have unilaterally incorporated the CEECs into their evolving system of co-operation in asylum and immigration matters, thereby re-introducing significant impediments to East-West migration and leading to a deep-rooted transformation of the international system of refugee protection. These processes are significant in three major ways. The first relates to the field of international relations and law and concerns the transformation of the international refugee regime. I will demonstrate that the extension of the current EU refugee regime, coupled with the general goal of combating illegal immigration, weakens the principles, norms and rules of international refugee protection by impeding the entry of asylum seekers and establishing a system of negative re-distribution for handling asylum claims.

Secondly, these processes are inherently linked to the question of European integration and the prospect of an Eastern enlargement of the Union. By highlighting the complex linkages between national and international developments in the field of asylum and immigration policies, this book provides new insights into the dynamics of 'Europeanisation' and illustrates the impact of member states' interests on the Union's attitude to Central and Eastern Europe. It will be shown that the fields of asylum and immigration, although not originally part of the EU agenda, now play an increasingly important role in the pre-accession strategies and may constitute significant obstacles to swift enlargement and the free movement of persons between the new and old member states.

Finally, the extension of restrictive asylum and immigration policies has important consequences for the CEECs them-

selves. Given that their adaptation to Western European policies has become a central condition for membership of the Union, the candidate countries face the conflicting requirement of
sealing their borders against illegal immigration whilst upholding
the humanitarian standards of refugee protection. These processes concern not only the approach of the CEECs to aliens
and immigration, but also affect the freedom of movement of
Central and Eastern European citizens and lead to the erection
of new borders in Europe.

This chapter introduces refugee policy as an international relations problem. The discussion of the basic normative and institutional elements of the international refugee regime provides the
contextual background for the analysis of the emergence and
extension of the EU refugee regime in successive chapters. It will
be shown that far from being a given concept, the notion of refugee protection has evolved constantly over time and has at all
times been significantly shaped by developments in the economic and political context of international co-operation. Given
the focus of this book on the countries of Central and Eastern
Europe and their adherence to the international refugee regime
today, a special emphasis is placed on the political friction that
split the international community into a Western and an Eastern
bloc and entailed the subsequent abstention of these states under the lead of the former Soviet Union from participation.

THE EMERGENCE OF THE INTERNATIONAL REGIME

Although the notion of 'asylum' as protection from persecution
can be traced back to the times of the Greeks and Romans
(Kimminich 1978: 7), its formal foundations were only laid in the
first half of the twentieth century when it was generally recognised that the refugee problem was a matter concerning the
international community and which needed to be addressed in
the context of international co-operation.

The Early Years of International Co-operation

The international codification of a refugee law must be seen in the context of the introduction of immigration controls in most European countries in the late nineteenth and early twentieth century. In contrast to the earlier open-border policy, refugees and migrants were no longer allowed to cross the borders without permission. The emergence of European nation states went along with the affirmation of a right to control the entry of non-nationals into their territory and the subsequent introduction of selective immigration rules. In the light of massive refugee movements produced by the Balkan Wars (1912–1913), World War I (1914–1918), and the Russian Revolution (1917), this closure of national borders could no longer be maintained. European states realised that some sort of legal status had to be given to these persons in order to allow them to move, stay, or return to their homes, legally.

Thus, initially, international co-operation for the protection of refugees concerned mainly the problem of stateless persons who had fled from their country without documents and who were without legal protection. In the literature, this period is referred to as the juridical or pragmatic phase of international co-operation (Hathaway 1984). At the behest of the overburdened International Committee of the Red Cross and other non-governmental organisations (NGOs), in 1921 the League of Nations appointed a High Commissioner for Russian Refugees in Europe, Fridjof Nansen–a move which constitutes the first formal acknowledgement of an international responsibility for refugees. The central achievement of the High Commissioner was the adoption of the 'Arrangement for the Issue of Certificates of Identity', the so-called 'Nansen passports' first awarded to Russian refugees (1922), and subsequently to Armenians (1924), Assyrians, Assyro-Chaldeans, Syrians, Kurds, and Turks (1928). The first non-group-specific agreement was concluded in 1933 and required the signatory states not to deny refugees access to their territories. However, this agreement was only ratified by eight countries, and with some significant restrictions.[1]

From 1935 onwards, a new perspective on refugee protection took shape, commonly referred to as the 'social' approach (Hathaway 1984). In this period, the earlier purely juridical criteria were supplemented by a factual perspective which established a group determination system based not only on the *de jure* loss of protection but also on *de facto* membership of a specific social group such as refugees fleeing from Germany, Austria or the Sudeten area of Czechoslovakia. At that time, refugees were granted recognition on the basis of group characteristics linked to their national origin and political events without individual status determination procedures. Although this group determination approach was never formally implemented in international refugee law, it has nevertheless continued to shape states' policies and is again gaining increasing importance today with respect to the massive movements of refugees fleeing from situations of generalised violence or civil war.

The foundations for the contemporary system of international refugee protection were laid at the end of the 1930s, commonly referred to as the 'individualist period'. It is important to note that this institutionalisation of the international refugee regime took place in an increasingly politicised environment, in which strategic considerations of security and foreign policy were to play a decisive role.

Tension between the League of Nations and the Soviet Union, which was not a member, was already evident in the 1920s when the latter raised strict objections to international efforts to help the thousands of defeated White Russian Army soldiers in the aftermath of the Russian Civil War (Loescher 1996: 38). At the same time, the need to find international solutions became increasingly evident with the dramatic intensification of the European refugee problem due to the spread of fascism and Nazism on the eve of World War II. While the Soviet Union continued to object to any kind of League protection for the few Russian citizens able to flee Stalin's dictatorship, Western European states were increasingly reluctant to commit themselves to the protection of Jews, in particular those fleeing Germany and its occupied territories.[2] By the end of World War

II, the refugee problem had reached dramatic proportions, relations between the Western powers and the Soviet Union rapidly deteriorated, and the issue of refugees became trapped in East-West controversies.

These controversies became manifest in the framework of the newly established United Nations, the heir of the League of Nations, when it addressed the refugee problem in its first general assembly. It was recognised that the refugee problem was 'international in scope and in nature' (UN quoted in Zarjevski 1988: 9), and led to the creation of an International Refugee Organisation (IRO), subsequently a focus of East-West tensions. The special committee responsible for drawing up a charter for the IRO comprised both refugee-receiving and refugee-sending countries which in 1946 were mainly those of the Eastern bloc.[3] The controversies between the two blocs centred around two questions. Firstly, the East opposed the idea that refugees could refuse repatriation and be resettled in another country. More specifically, the Soviets and the Yugoslavs claimed that persons who were hostile to their governments should not receive support from the other member states of the UN (Kimminich 1978: 54), which constituted a clear denial of the notion of political asylum. The second point of controversy concerned the definition of a refugee. Focussing on Soviet dissidents, the West insisted that the IRO mandate should be broad enough to cover individuals with 'valid objections' to repatriation, including the fear of persecution. In contrast to the earlier practice of refugee status determination guided by group categories and following national or territorial criteria, in this period one can observe a clear shift to an individual determination based on the notion of persecution for specific reasons such as race, religion, or political beliefs which attest an existential conflict between the refugee and his or her government. In the end, the IRO charter was drafted by the Western majority in conscious opposition to the Eastern bloc (Kimminich 1978: 54; Glahn 1992: 70). It is in this context that today's definition of a refugee, based on individual criteria rather than the risk of general violence, must be understood. As a consequence of this approach, Eastern European countries refused to join the new organisation and started to regard it as 'an instrument of the Western bloc' in its fight against Communism.[4]

The East-West conflict continued to overshadow the construction of the international refugee regime in the United Nations system. The IRO's mandate was initially limited to the consequences of World War II, but this was soon extended to include refugees from Eastern European Communist regimes, as in the case of Czechoslovakia after the Communist coup in 1948. In the West, refugees became a symbol of Soviet repression and were used by governments as instruments of 'cold war' antagonism (Loescher 1996: 51).

It was in this hostile atmosphere,[5] and against the votes from the Eastern bloc, that the General Assembly decided to establish the Office of the United Nations High Commissioner for Refugees (UNHCR) in 1949.[6] Although this office was initially designed to resolve only the problem of residual refugees following the cessation of the mandate of the IRO, contrary to the will of some West European states,[7] it has remained the central international organisation for the promotion of refugee protection. Its statute defines the range of persons who fall under its mandate and the substance of protection. This includes principally the promotion of international conventions for the protection of refugees and the supervision of their implementation and revision. It was under its auspices that the central principles, norms, rules and procedures of the international refugee regime became institutionalised.[8]

Normative and Institutional Provisions

The term 'international regimes' was developed in international relations theory and commonly refers to a set of 'principles, norms and decision-making procedures around which actor expectations converge in a given issue area.' (Krasner 1982: 185). They can be described as formal and informal international institutions which guide international co-operation over problems of mutual concern. Legally speaking, the international system of political asylum is situated at the interface between state sovereignty and universal human rights. On the one hand, the principle of the sovereign equality of states, forming the basis of international relations,[9] entitles every state to unilaterally regulate the conditions of the entry, stay and exit of aliens on its territory. On the other hand, this sovereignty is limited by universal principles of human rights and human dignity which have gained normative status especially since their codification in international law in the first half of the twentieth century.

In formal terms, the international refugee regime is governed by three different bodies of international law which relate to the principle of asylum: statutory refugee law, human rights' law and, albeit to a lesser extent, humanitarian law. The actual asylum practice, and accordingly the level of international protection, are, however, highly contingent on the domestic implementation mechanisms at the level of the nation states. Hence, a realistic assessment of the basic instruments of the international refugee regime must consider both formal principles and actual practice.

THE FORMAL BASIS: THE GENEVA CONVENTION AND THE DEFINITION OF A REFUGEE

The primary source of refugee law is the Geneva Convention relating to the Status of Refugees of 1951 together with the New York Protocol of 1967. The convention, which was prepared by the UNHCR, was initially limited to persons who became refugees as a result of events occurring before 1 January 1951, with an optional geographical limitation to events occurring within Europe. It was designed to regulate the organisation of the right to asylum, or rather, to establish the minimum standards to be applied by contracting states with regard to, for example, the right to work or the right to education, and provides for the basic protection required by asylum seekers and refugees. The Preamble to the Geneva Convention grounds refugee law in the universal principles of human rights, invoking international solidarity, co-operation and burden-sharing. In Article 1, the Convention defines the term 'refugee' as 'any person who, owing to a well-founded fear of being persecuted for reasons of race, religion, nationality, membership of a particular social group or political opinion, is outside the country of his nationality and is unable or, owing to such fear, unwilling to avail himself of the protection of that country'. With this definition, the UN community upheld the individual concept of a refugee developed in the late 1930s in contrast to a broader notion based on group characteristics. The fact that, at the time when the Convention was being drafted, the overwhelming majority of persons in need of international protection had fled their countries of origin because of generalised violence or had been deported suggests that the UN community was eager to limit the scope of the emergent international regime, and 'to make the status of refugee exceptional, so as to preclude overwhelming numbers.' (Zolberg, Surhke and Aguayo 1989: 25). The temporal and the geographical limitation to the convention's scope are also indicative of a reluctance to take on a far-reaching commitment to refugee protection at the international level.

In addition to the definition of refugee as per the international refugee regime, this book uses the following terms. Persons wishing to apply for refugee status and to formally submit an asylum claim are referred to as 'asylum seekers'. Once a person has been recognised under this formal procedure and granted refugee status, the terms 'recognised refugee' or 'person granted asylum' are used. In this sense, 'refugees' can refer to both asylum seekers and other forced migrants who do not apply for the formal status determination procedure. The term 'immigrants' is used for voluntary migrants.

THE RIGHT OF ASYLUM: RIGHTS OF THE INDIVIDUAL VERSUS THE RIGHT OF THE STATE

In drafting the Geneva Convention, national governments refused to implement a legal obligation on states to provide asylum in the form of a subjective right of the refugee to receive asylum. The provisions of the Geneva Convention instead presuppose the assignment and execution of refugee status as the prerogative of the sovereign contracting states. Such a binding obligation had already been seriously discussed a few years earlier in the context of the negotiations leading up to the Universal Declaration of Human Rights adopted in 1948. While a first draft of the declaration contained the provision that 'everyone has the right to seek and be granted, in other countries, asylum from persecution',[10] the final version (Art. 14) refers to the 'right to seek and enjoy' asylum and thus returned to the primacy of state sovereignty.

In order to strengthen the international obligations of states *vis-à-vis* refugees, both the United Nations and the Council of Europe tried to reach an agreement on the codification of an individual right of asylum after the adoption of the Geneva Convention. In the United Nations, the efforts to provide such a right in an internationally binding convention on human rights began immediately after the above mentioned declaration and went on until 1966.[11] In the end, it was decided to detach asylum law from human rights law and to draw up a separate convention on territorial asylum leading to the United Nations Declaration on Territorial Asylum in 1967.[12] Contrary to initial expectations, however, this declaration merely confirmed the right of states to grant asylum.

A similar development took place in the European context. The European Convention on Human Rights and Fundamental Freedoms of 1950 makes no mention of asylum, and a first attempt to include asylum was instead made in a statement of the Consultative Assembly of the Council of Europe to the Council of Ministers in 1961 which proposed to insert a substantive right to asylum in the second protocol of the convention. After the failure of this initiative, a second and last attempt was made with the Convention on Territorial Asylum adopted by the member states of the Council of Europe on 5 December 1977. Yet once again, asylum was confirmed as a prerogative of the state.

Thus, the international refugee regime is still based on the sovereign right of states to grant asylum rather than a right of the refugee to be granted asylum–a condition which makes it highly dependent on the receiving states' commitment.

While there is a marked variation in the domestic implementation of asylum regulations across Western states, it often went beyond international obligations and took a more assertive stance. Several European states adopted the principle of asylum in their national constitutions, and some, such as the Federal Republic of Germany and France, formulated it as an individual subjective right.[13]

THE LIMITATION OF SOVEREIGNTY AND THE NORM OF NON-REFOULEMENT

Apart from the removal of the original time and place limitations of the Geneva Conventions with the New York Protocol in 1967,[14] the formal scope of the international refugee regime was not extended any further. Nevertheless, the regime's practical scope was *de facto* broadened through the application of the norm of non-refoulement provided in the convention. This norm is laid down in Article 33 of the Geneva Convention of 1951 which stipulates that, 'No Contracting State shall expel or return ('refouler') a refugee in any manner whatsoever to the frontiers of territories where his life or freedom would be threatened on account of his race, religion, nationality, membership of a particular social group or political opinion'.

This norm of non-refoulement represents the central limit posed by human rights considerations upon states' prerogative to decide on the entry and stay of persons in need of protection. Over the years, it has gained the status of a principle of customary international law, which means that it is considered universally binding on all states irrespective of their assent to the convention (Goodwill-Gill 1995).[15] This informal extension can be interpreted as an attempt 'to deal with the humanitarian reality of refugee movements' (Goodwin-Gill 1995: 9), which contrasts with the restrictive interpretation of the refugee definition. Thus, the crucial norm of the international refugee regime today is not the right to asylum as such, but the obligation of states not to return people demanding protection to countries where they would risk serious human rights violations.

This central principle of asylum law is reinforced by general human rights law and, to a lesser extent, by humanitarian law. At the international level, the prohibition of refoulement is provided in the International Covenant on Civil and Political Rights of 1966,[16] and the 1984 United Nations Declaration against Torture and Other Cruel Inhuman or Degrading Treatment or Punishment.[17] At the European level, such a prohibition is contained in the European Convention on Human Rights and Fundamental Freedoms.[18]

It is important to note that today, the range of persons protected by the prohibition of refoulement is much broader than the definition of refugees under the Geneva Convention. The acceptance of non-Convention refugees by the host countries of the West usually occurs on a relatively unformalised and *ad hoc* basis, where they are variously classified as '*bona fide* refugees', the 'externally displaced', '*de facto*' or 'humanitarian' refugees. In the absence of a set of international rules, their status is very disparate throughout Europe and does not, by and large, award the same quality of rights and conditions for settlement as per the Geneva Convention.[19]

In practice, this means that the international refugee regime today builds on two different legal categories of persons in need of protection. On the one hand, there are individual refugees who are granted asylum because they are persecuted on the grounds of their race, religion, nationality, or membership of a particular social or political group. On the other, there is the broad majority of forced migrants who do not strictly fulfil these criteria but who cannot be sent back because of humanitarian considerations.[20] However, neither the formal definition nor the *de facto* notion of refugees is interpreted in a unitary or even a consensual manner by either decision-makers or academics.[21]

In sum, three principles constitute the contemporary international refugee regime: the principle of asylum as the lasting protection of persons fleeing from individual human rights violations, while the 'right' to grant asylum remains the prerogative of the state; the principle of non-refoulement which, derived from universal human rights considerations, broadens the categories of persons to be admitted to a territory and thereby limits the scope of states' sovereignty; and the principle of international co-operation and solidarity and the principle of implementation in national law.

Having established the basic normative and institutional elements of the international refugee regime, the following section presents a short overview of its evolution with reference to changes in the configuration of the global refugee problem.

THE EVOLUTION OF REFUGEE PROTECTION: BETWEEN CHANGE AND STAGNATION

The evolution of the international refugee regime from its institutionalisation until the present day can be roughly divided into the following four phases:

- a liberal phase of refugee policy in the 1950s, consisting mainly of the repatriation of World War II refugees and the protection of refugees from Central and Eastern Europe;
- a shift of the refugee problem to countries of the Third World in the 1960s;
- the introduction of first administrative reforms in Western asylum policies after the general halt on labour immigration in the early 1970s;

- the comprehensive re-orientation of refugee policies starting in the mid-1980s.

The fourth, and still current, phase is characterised by the introduction of restrictive reforms at the national level and the search for co-ordinated solutions at the European level. Triggered by increasing numbers of asylum-seekers and the end of the 'cold war', these efforts lead to the implementation of a regional European refugee regime which redefines the traditional principles, norms and rules of refugee protection.[22]
This chapter presents an overview over the first three phases of international co-operation, whilst the fourth phase, which touches mainly on the transformation of European asylum policies, is dealt with in Chapters 2 and 3.

Phase One: The European Refugee Problem

From the genesis of the international refugee regime, one can assume that, at the moment of its institutionalisation, the perception of the refugee problem was limited to events that had occurred in Europe. Indeed, for most of the 1950s refugees came almost exclusively from Central and Eastern Europe to seek asylum in the West. The persecution-centred refugee definition of the Geneva Convention accurately reflected the situation of many of these East European exiles. As their numbers increased, Communist governments started to regard this emigration as an offence against their ideological contentions and condemned it as crime against the state. They introduced barriers to emigration and imposed drastic sentences on clandestine exit. On the other hand, Western governments welcomed and encouraged these emigrations 'in order to weaken their rivals ideologically and to gain political legitimacy in their cold war struggle' (Loescher 1996: 59). Notably the United States and the Federal Republic of Germany with respect to East Germany combined their foreign policy objectives with liberal asylum practices.[23] The preparedness of the West to support anti-

Communist dissidents is illustrated in their reaction to the massive refugee flows produced by the Soviet invasion of Hungary in November 1956. Without examining their eligibility under the Geneva Convention, Western governments lowered their barriers to immigration and provided immediate resettlement opportunities for nearly 200,000 Hungarian refugees in less than two years (Loescher 1996: 68ff.).

Similarly, in the case of Czechoslovakia in 1968, the practice of individual examination of applications was waived in favour of an informal group-determination procedure.

This solidarity of Western European governments with Eastern and Central European dissidents is exemplified in the case of the Federal Republic of Germany. Here, a general rule was adopted in 1966 which stipulated that asylum-seekers from the Eastern bloc who had been denied refugee status should not be returned to their countries of origin.[24] This policy was only abandoned for Hungarian asylum-seekers in 1987 and for other Eastern Europeans in 1989 (Münch 1992: 61). This liberal approach to refugees in the first phase of the international refugee regime was supported by a dynamic economic environment which favoured not only generosity towards refugees, but also supported the intake of large numbers of labour migrants in all Western European countries.

Phase Two: The Dislocation of the Refugee Problem

The second phase of the international refugee regime was introduced in the early 1960s with a profound transformation in the configuration of the international refugee problem. On the one hand, ever fewer Central and Eastern Europeans applied for asylum in the West, partly in consequence of the erection of emigration barriers by the Communist governments. On the other hand, the locus of forced migration passed to the Third World, where anti-colonial insurgency and general violence following the rapid decolonialisation generated vast numbers of refugees.[25] This second phase lasted until the mid-1970s and is characterised by the combination of a dynamic environment leading to a *de facto* extension of the categories of persons benefiting from international protection, and stagnation of policy responses in Western European countries. Whereas the structure of the international refugee problem changed both quantitatively and qualitatively, Western states, virtually untouched by these new developments, continued to pursue mainly liberal and informal policies in an atmosphere of flourishing economies.

The transformation of the refugee problem started with the outbreak of decolonisation and secession struggles in Africa and India,[26] which produced sudden and violent outflows of millions of people. During the 1960s, it is assumed that the African continent hosted more than 1 million refugees (Zolberg, Surhke and Aguayo 1989), and the number of persons uprooted by the short but violent Bengali war in northeast India has been estimated at 5–9 million (Suhrke 1993: 217).

Although these millions of refugees remained mainly in their regions of origin and did not reach European states, their presence posed a challenge to the instruments of the international refugee regime as institutionalised after World War II. The majority of these people did not fulfil the criteria of a refugee under the 1951 Geneva Convention. They were either victims of generalised violence or participants in mass movements rather than being subject to individual persecution, and the reasons for their flight could not be related to events which had occurred prior to 1951. Thus, the international refugee regime had to adapt to these new categories of refugees.

In a first step, the mandate of the UNHCR was extended in 1961 to include other persons under a 'good offices' doctrine.[27] Secondly, on the initiative of this organisation, the international community agreed on the above mentioned protocol to the Geneva Convention signed in New York in 1967 which abolished the deadline of January 1951 and relinquished the geographical limitation for all states wishing to do so.[28] In Africa and Latin America, regional refugee definitions were adopted, which far exceeded the limited scope of the individual-based definition of persecution in the Geneva Convention. As a sign of the liberal attitude prevailing towards refugees in most countries at that time, the New York Protocol was ratified very rapidly by a large number of governments not party to the original Geneva Convention.[29]

In this period, the ground was laid for one of the major challenges of today's refugee regime. The scope of international protection was *de facto* extended to a vaguely defined variety of persons suffering 'relevant harm' in their country of origin (Goodwin-Gill 1995). However, 'the inadequacies of the prevailing system did not become apparent until the 1980s, when deteriorating political conditions, increasing ethnic and religious tensions, proliferating internal conflicts, and growing East-West tensions in the Third World generated massive outpourings of refugees who sought political asylum in the industrialised nations.' (Loescher 1996: 81).

Phase Three: The Reorientation of European Asylum Policies

Two developments brought an end to liberal refugee policy and the onset of a third phase of international co-operation–the economic recession of the early 1970s; and the globalisation of the refugee problem leading to an increase of non-European asylum seekers in Europe. A significant step in Europe's reorientation *vis-à-vis* refugee matters was made with the general stop put to labour immigration in the aftermath of the 1972/73 oil crisis. This had two impacts on asylum policies. Firstly, when immigration rules were still generous, many persons forced to leave their country of origin because of persecution or other human rights violations did not necessarily apply for asylum if other ways of entering the country were available. Secondly, these restrictions revealed a basic contradiction in the refugee system itself: whereas before, refugees who did not fulfil the criteria laid down in the Geneva Convention were usually accepted under immigration law, governments now had to find new ways of either returning them to their countries of origin, or, with the risk of refoulement, providing another basis for their stay. After the abolition of economic migration schemes, asylum became the only legal avenue to enter Western European states apart from family reunification.

Parallel to the economic recession, the 1970s mark the beginning of a globalisation of the refugee problem. The multiplication of causes and regions of origin, and, in contrast to the 1960s, the multiplication of flows and an increase in overall mobility and information led to the direct exposure of industrialised countries. In this third phase of the international regime, Western Europe started to question its hitherto liberal admission policies and to introduce restrictive measures.

A major source of refugee flows in this decade originated in the internationalisation of liberation struggles in the developing world. Two major international crises carried the 'new' refugees to European borders: the spread of repressive military regimes in South America,[30] and the protracted conflicts in Indo-China producing innumerable refugees, especially after 1975. In addition, conflicts in South Africa and the Horn of Africa, Ethiopia, Central America and Afghanistan after the Soviet invasion radicalised the refugee crisis of the 1970s.

This crisis posed new challenges to the international community. In contrast to earlier refugee flows in the Third World, these refugees did not remain within their region of origin but made their way to the industrialised countries. Given the impossibility of repatriation due to continuous tensions in their country of origin, they needed long-term resettlement in asylum countries. While during the 1970s, only select refugee groups were accepted on a quota basis,[31] the end of the decade marked the arrival of increasing numbers of spontaneous refugees, which, in the eyes of the governments, undermined their sovereign power to control immigration. In this period, a growing opposition of Western countries to generous admission policies emerged, and administrative restrictions on asylum procedures were introduced. In the Federal Republic of Germany, political debate raised the question of the possible abuse of asylum law. As a consequence visa requirements were imposed on several refugee-producing countries and administrative reforms were introduced to relieve domestic asylum procedures from 1977 onwards (Wolken 1988: 44ff.; Münch 1992). In France, a debate started on immigration, integration, racism and multiculturalism, which, given the rising numbers of asylum-seekers, was slowly extended to include refugees and led to a policy of dissuasion based on a restriction of procedural rights and a limitation of recognition rates.[32] Denmark, Belgium, and the Netherlands soon followed suit with a wave of restrictive measures marking a shift in policy orientation.[33]

This trend became equally salient at the European level. Here, the failure to adopt a substantive right to asylum in the Council of Europe's Declaration on Territorial Asylum of 1977 is indicative of a reluctance to strengthen the international commitment to refugee protection. This tendency was confirmed in the United Nations framework when, in 1980, a preventive approach was launched on the initiative from the Federal Republic of Germany, in order to avert new flows of refugees.[34]

These changes are all indicative of the situation of international co-operation in refugee matters from the mid-1980s to the present day. During the 1980s, deteriorating political conditions, increasing ethnic and religious tensions, proliferating internal conflicts, and growing East-West tensions in Third World countries generated massive flows of refugees seeking asylum in the industrialised world. During the second half of the 1970s, the global refugee population amounted to between 2.4 and 4.6 million persons, whereas in 1983 their number had increased to over 10 million and continued to rise steadily to a total of 18.2 million in 1993. In 1995 the numbers had decreased to a total of 14.4 million refugees.[35] Accordingly, while more than 90 per cent of the refugees world-wide remain outside Europe, the numbers of asylum-seekers in Western Europe increased from 65,400 in 1983 to a peak of 692,683 in 1992, before dropping to 318,887 in 1994.[36]

Faced with these developments, European governments increasingly began to question their ability to control immigration into their territories and started to place restrictions on their asylum regulations. Furthermore, in the European Union, the issues of immigration and asylum were put on the agenda of intergovernmental negotiations linked to the Single Market project designed to relieve domestic asylum procedures and to limit the intake of asylum seekers in the member states.

The end of the 'cold war' and the ensuing internal and external conflicts do not represent a turning point as such but, from an analytical point of view, rather the significant amplification of existing trends. Both a radicalised refugee burden and the insecurity about further developments supplied those who were in favour of far-reaching restrictions with legitimacy and urgency, so that since the 1990s a limitation of the asylum system became an uncontested claim in all Western European governments.

CONCLUSION

The review of the history of the international refugee regime generates three major insights: the quantitative broadening of the scope of the international refugee regime due to a multiplication of the causes and the numbers of refugees; the qualitative extension of the range of persons qualifying as refugees under various categories; and the stagnation of national asylum policies in Western countries. While the first two observations refer to the structure of the refugee problem itself, the third concerns the aspect of political, legal and institutional responses. The major contradiction of today's refugee regime becomes obvious: a dynamic evolution of its basic concerns faced by a stagnation of its formal operational instruments.

This paradoxical mismatch raises the fundamental questions: 'Who deserves international protection?', 'What is the basis of an international responsibility?' and 'Where are the limits of sovereignty'? A short discussion of the structural transformations of the global refugee problem underpins these questions empirically and helps clarify the major challenges to the international refugee regime today.

The question 'who' is a refugee has changed constantly depending on political interests, available legal instruments, and empirical realities without ever having been defined or applied in a consistent manner.[37] The legal and institutional framework of the contemporary international refugee regime was established in the early 1950s. In the context of intensifying East-West rivalries, it was shaped to respond to the needs of individual political dissidents. Since the 1960s, we can observe a clear multiplication of causes of refugee flows. Whereas at the time of the drafting of the Geneva Convention, the scope of international protection was limited to events of a genuinely political nature which had occurred before 1951, today's refugee regime applies to a whole range of different causes of human rights violations. The reason for the international community's failure to recognise these changes is, at least in part, due to the special dynamics of the 'cold war'. While the Western states continued to reduce their perception to political causes rooted in the existence of totalitarian regimes, Communist and many developing countries denounced colonialism, global economic inequality, and racial discrimination as the major sources of forced migration.[38] It was not until the end of systemic and ideological animosity between East and West that the multiple political, historical, sociological, economic and ecological causes of refugee movements started to win recognition.[39]

The primary source of refugee flows is war. Once limited to Third World countries, the reality of war has now returned to the European continent after the dissolution of the Soviet Union and Yugoslavia. The legacies of colonialism and the crises of integration and disintegration due to the arbitrary delineation of territorial boundaries regardless of ethnic, religious and racial distinctions, struggles over political influence and resources, fights for self-determination and independence, the militarisation of Third World countries under superpower rivalry, and the instability of administrative structures in newly independent states are all factors contributing to the emergence of violent inter-state and intra-state conflict (Zolberg, Surhke and Aguayo 1989). A second major source of forced migration is the persistence of dictatorial regimes in different parts of the world and the related political persecution of dissidents and the oppression of ethnic or religious minorities striving for political autonomy or separatism. In contrast to these forms of 'man-made' persecution, a relatively new cause of forced migration now recognised as a challenge by the international community is natural disasters such as floods, earthquakes, or drought, which, linked to the problem of over-population, deprive an ever increasing number of persons of their livelihood. Finally, at a global systemic level, growing economic cleavages between rich and poor countries are increasingly seen as a direct or indirect cause of repression and violence, and thereby an additional source of refugee flows.

The review of these 'objective' causes, however, does not necessarily provide the answer to the question posed above. From a critical point of view, it appears that the issue of who qualifies as a refugee is a function of political and legal considerations. This conclusion is supported by a review of statistical data on asylum-seekers, refugees, and recognition rates in the various host countries. While recognition rates might serve as an indicator for the question, 'Who is a refugee?', an international comparison reveals the inherent contradictions of the contemporary refugee regime. For example, in 1992, the overall recognition rates of refugees obtaining the status of the Geneva Convention varied between 3.2 per cent in the UK, to 4.2 per cent in Germany and 28 per cent in France. At the same time, however, the UK granted 43.9 per cent of asylum-seekers another status to remain based on the rule of non-refoulement and Germany 20.1 per cent (Intergovernmental Consultations 1995: 313). When broken down in national categories, the comparability of recognition rates becomes even more questionable. In the case of asylum seekers from Sri Lanka, for instance, in

1989 Germany recognised less than 1 per cent under Convention status, while France accepted approximately 64 per cent and Canada as much as 96 per cent (Arboleda and Hoy 1993: 81). In sum, the data underline the absence of a common background of structural legal criteria determining who qualifies as a refugee and indicate that the definition is a function of states' sovereign considerations.[40]

This lack of clarity and the profound disagreement over the basic categories of the international refugee regime lead us to the second question regarding the international responsibility of states to protect refugees. Although the international refugee regime conceives of the duty to grant asylum mainly as a prerogative of the nation states, the ability of the latter to reject refugees at their borders is severely limited not only by their national legislation, but also by international human rights' norms and, in particular, the norm of non-refoulement. As a consequence, nation states are not free to control their intake of refugees, a fact deplored by all industrialised countries as indicative of a loss of sovereignty over this category of immigrants. As a consequence, the need to reform the contemporary system of refugee protection has become an evident challenge in the eyes of both national governments and international organisations. In Western Europe, the main refugee receiving countries started to restrict their national regulations and initiated a process of intergovernmental co-ordination for the formulation of common responses, analysed in Chapter 2.

NOTES

1. 'Convention Relating to the International Status of Refugees' of 28 October 1933, ratified by Belgium, Bulgaria, Denmark, France, Italy, Norway, Czechoslovakia and the United Kingdom, see Kimminich (1978: 51–52).

2. This reluctance became particularly salient in the course of the Conference in Evian 1938, which represents the only significant effort to find an international solution to the problem of Jewish refugees. However, the participating countries merely established a non-committal Intergovernmental

Committee on Refugees (IGCR) to negotiate with Germany about Jewish migration, which had little impact (see Sjøberg 1991).

3. Spain was an exception.

4. For the relevance of the East-West conflict for the evolution of the international refugee regime, see Salomon (1991).

5. In addition to the Communist seizure of Czechoslovakia, key events which contributed to the deterioration of East-West relations were the Berlin crisis, the victory of Mao Tse-tung in China, and the onset of the Korean conflict in 1950.

6. UN General Assembly Resolution 319 of 3 December 1949.

7. In particular France and Belgium, see Loescher (1996: 56).

8. The term 'international refugee regime' refers to the Western regime rooted in the UN system, in contrast to other regional regimes such as those found in Africa or Latin America.

9. See Art. 2, para. 1 of the UN Charter.

10. Art. 12 of the Draft Universal Declaration of Human Rights, UN Document E/800.

11. UN document E/CN 4/L 184 and 191; E/CN 4/713; see also *International Law Association Reports*, Tokyo Conference (1964: 285ff.).

12. UN General Assembly Resolution 2312/XXII, General Assembly Official Records, 22nd Session, Supplement No. 16.

13. The Federal Republic of Germany in Art. 16 of the *Grundgesetz* and France in the Preamble of its Constitution.

14. For an account of the developments leading up to this decision, see the following section.

15. There is an increasing trend among jurists to consider the principle of non-refoulement as a peremptory norm of international law from which no derogation is permitted (*ius cogens*) (ECRE 1993: 18).

16. Art. 13 of the International Covenant on Civil and Political Rights, adopted and opened for signature, ratification and accession by General Assembly Resolution 2200 A (XXI) of 16 December 1966.

17. Art. 3 of the UN Declaration against Torture and Other Cruel Inhuman or Degrading Treatment or Punishment, adopted and opened for signature, ratification and accession by General Assembly Resolution 39/46 of 10 December 1984.

18. Especially Art. 3 of the European Convention on Human Rights and Fundamental Freedoms, signed in Rome on 4 November 1950. But also Art. 8 (the right to private and family life), and Art. 13 (the right to an 'effective remedy before a national authority') provide protection against refoulement.

19. Most Western countries have implemented a special status for these refugees who do not fall under the Geneva Convention, e.g. the 'B Status' in Scandinavian countries, 'exceptional leave to remain' in Britain, and '*Duldung*' or temporary status in Germany (see Hailbronner 1993).

20. In contrast to the limited definition of the international refugee regime, a broader notion of the refugee has been adopted in regional agreements in Africa and South America. In 1969, the Convention of the Organisation of African Unity defined a refugee as 'every person who, owing to external aggression, occupation, foreign domination or events seriously disturbing public order in either part or the whole of his country of origin or nationality, is compelled to leave his place of habitual residence in order to seek refuge in another place outside his country of origin or nationality'. Similarly, the 1984 Cartagena Declaration by the Organisation of American States defines refugees in collective terms as 'persons who have fled their country because their lives, safety or freedom have been threatened by generalised violence, foreign aggression, internal conflicts, massive violation of human rights or other circumstances which have seriously disturbed the public order'.

21. For a discussion of the problems of interpretation of the refugee definition see Goodwin-Gill 1995; Hathaway 1991a; Arboleda and Hoy 1993. See also the conclusion to this chapter.

22. This classification tries to combine an assessment of the structural changes of the refugee problem with a policy perspective focusing on Western European responses.

23. See Salomon (1991) for the United States and Wolken (1988) for the Federal Republic of Germany.

24. Unpublished decision by the Conference of the Permanent Conference of the Interior Ministers of the *Länder,* see Münch (1992: 60).

25. For a comprehensive analysis of refugee movements in the Third World, see Zolberg, Surhke and Aguayo (1989).

26. These were the decolonialisation struggles in Algeria (starting in 1959), Zaire (1960), Rwanda (1963), Portuguese Africa (circa 1961), the confrontation between North and South in Sudan around 1963, and the secession war in Bengali (northeast India).

27. UN General Assembly Resolution 1673 (XVI) of 18 December 1961.

28. 'Protocol Relating to the Status of Refugees' of 31 January 1967, UN Treaty, 606: 267.

29. According to Holborn, the number of accessions and ratifications to both the 1951 Convention and the 1967 Protocol almost quadrupled between 1960 and 1970 (Holborn 1975: 199ff.).

30. These were the overthrow of the Allende government in Chile in 1973, and the military takeovers in Uruguay in 1972 and Argentina in 1976.

31. This was especially the case for refugees from Indo-China and Chile (Zolberg, Surhke and Aguayo 1989).

32. In 1973 the number of asylum seekers totalled 1,620, but this figure rose to 18,000 in 1976 (Teitgen-Colly 1994: 97; Noiriel 1991; Weil 1991).

33. For a comparative account of Western European asylum policies, see Hailbronner (1989) and Heinelt (1994).

34. Soon after, the 'UN Group of Governmental Experts on International Co-operation to avert new flows of refugees' was established to formulate a joint strategy of flight prevention. While this project had little impact at that time, it is gaining increasing importance in contemporary efforts to contain the refugee problem (Lee 1986).

35. These numbers are taken from UNHCR (1995a: 248) which shows an annual worldwide increase of 1 million refugees from 1981 to 1993.

36. Taken from UNHCR (1995a: 253).

37. Arboleda and Hoy (1993: 76), former UNHCR officers, come to a similar conclusion when they call for more specific criteria and a uniform application of the refugee definition. From an academic point of view, Hathaway shares this concern (Hathaway 1991a: 114).

38. See Suhrke (1993: 219) with reference to the debate on 'root causes' in the United Nations starting in 1980.

39. The argument that today's refugee causes are not new is illustrated in a 1981 report issued by the former UN High Commissioner for Refugees, the Aga Khan, in which he integrated both the political and economic factors invoked by the UN member states plus the following factors: the availability of firearms, the pressure on resources associated with high population growth, massive unemployment, large rural-to-urban migrations, and desertification (Suhrke 1993: 219–20).

40. According to Joly (1996), the political construction of asylum is a function of domestic and foreign policy considerations supplemented by ethical factors.

2 The Emergence of the EU Refugee Regime

In the aftermath of the 'cold war', the idea of refugee protection has become an increasingly contested issue in international relations. Western European states have all followed a common trend invoking a 'crisis' of the asylum system by carrying out restrictive reforms of their asylum laws and limiting access to their territories for asylum seekers and voluntary migrants alike.

Although these changes are often presented as a direct reaction to increasing numbers of asylum seekers and refugees and the increasingly xenophobic nature of public opinion, they do not occur in an isolated manner but are part of the institutionalisation of a regional refugee regime in the European Union that redefines the principles and rules of the traditional system of refugee protection.[1] In contrast to the widely held opinion that this restrictive trend was induced by the opening up of the Eastern bloc and the collapse of the old bipolar system, with the consequent fear of massive refugee flows world-wide, the about turn in Western European refugee policies had already started in the mid-1980s and was immediately linked to the process of European integration.

By taking a longitudinal perspective we can retrace the history of co-operation among Western European countries in refugee matters and examine the specific European dimension of these changes. Therefore, the first section examines an earlier attempt to harmonise EU asylum policies, which were not linked with the process of European integration but which were promoted by the Council of Europe, before turning to the evolution of today's emergent EU refugee regime. The intergovernmental negotiations among EU member states laying the foundations of this regime with the Schengen and the Dublin Conventions are discussed in following section. The analysis goes on to examine the evolution of this co-operation between the Maastricht and Amsterdam Treaty on the European Union, and the chapter ends with a synopsis of the normative and institutional framework of this emergent EU refugee regime.

CO-OPERATION IN THE COUNCIL OF EUROPE

Long before the issues of asylum and immigration were placed on the EU agenda, the Council of Europe raised the question of co-operation among the member states and proposed the harmonisation of national asylum policies.[2] The general aim underlying these activities was the implementation of the Geneva Convention and related human rights treaties in Europe and the steady improvement of the situation of asylum seekers and refugees. These efforts culminated in a proposal to establish a system of European co-operation for handling asylum claims which, while putting much more emphasis on human rights, would have strong links with the intergovernmental agreements reached among the EU member states a few years later.

Although these initiatives of the Council of Europe did not really influence the development of the ensuing EU refugee regime, they highlight the broader international context of co-operation in this field. Furthermore, these activities have again been gaining increasing importance in recent years with the accession of new member states from Eastern and Central Europe to the Council of Europe,[3] and their participation in the international refugee regime (see Chapter 3).

The Council of Europe first broached the issue of refugees in the 1960s. Placing special emphasis on the protection of human rights, the Committee of Ministers adopted a resolution in 1967 which provided that governments 'should act in a particularly liberal and humanitarian spirit in relation to persons who seek asylum on their territory' and should co-operate 'in a spirit of European solidarity and of common responsibility in this field'.[4] In 1976, the Parliamentary Assembly raised for the first time the issue of harmonising the national interpretations of the refugee definition of the Geneva Convention.[5] A second recommendation of the same year addressed the situation of refugees who did not fulfil the criteria of the Geneva Convention but who were accepted on humanitarian grounds.[6]

Shortly after the failure of the UN conference on territorial asylum in 1977, the Committee of Ministers adopted a 'Declaration on Territorial Asylum' to affirm the positive attitude of its member states towards the principle of asylum.[7] In the same year, the Ad Hoc Committee of Experts on the Legal Aspects of Refugees (CAHAR) was established. This committee is made up of governmental experts and formulates legal instruments for discussion and adoption by the Council of Ministers. The idea behind its creation was that the international refugee problem constituted a common concern for European states and thus required a certain degree of harmonisation of legal standards (Hailbronner 1989: 27). This harmonisation was designed to improve the situation of asylum seekers and refugees in Europe and to fight the phenomenon of 'refugees in orbit', defined as 'persons who, although they have not been placed in immediate jeopardy by being rejected at the frontier or otherwise sent back to the country where they are liable to persecution, are not granted asylum, still less refugee status, in any country in which they make an application for asylum.' (Melander 1978). In short, it refers to refugees unable to find a state willing to examine their asylum request.

In 1981, the Committee of Ministers adopted a recommendation on the harmonisation of national asylum procedures. This sets out the principles governments should apply in dealing with asylum requests.[8] These are to ensure 'fundamental guarantees to be granted to asylum seekers' and the minimal standards for determination procedures. The standards include the permission of the applicant to remain in the territory of the state while his demand is examined; referral of the decision to a central authority; objective and impartial judgement; and clear instructions to immigration officers regarding non-refoulement. While this recommendation did not deal with the substantive criteria for granting refugee status, a far-reaching harmonisation was proposed in a recommendation made by the Parliamentary Assembly in 1985, where the member states were requested to harmonise their substantive criteria for asylum and the aims of effective co-operation and burden-sharing were set forth.[9] To this end, national asylum policies were to be standardised. In particular, the following measures were recommended: the elaboration of a European convention on determination procedures and substantive interpretation of eligibility criteria, and, particularly important with regard to the future of European co-operation, the adoption of a common definition of the concept of 'first country of asylum' determining the responsibility of one specific member state for the examination of an asylum claim. This measure was designed to improve both European co-operation and the standards of refugee protection and to counter the phenomenon of 'refugees in orbit' by fixing a responsibility on states and thereby ensuring the examination of each individual asylum claim.

A first attempt to agree on a common determination of responsibility rules within the Council of Europe failed in 1984 because of major differences between the traditional transit countries and the countries of asylum.[10] In particular, states which perceived themselves as countries of transit for refugees, such as Turkey, Italy and Greece,[11] feared that these rules might entail a dislocation of refugee movements to their debit (Hailbronner 1989: 30; Loescher 1989: 628–29). Nevertheless, under pressure from major receiving countries, especially Germany, the efforts to draft such an agreement were soon renewed and entailed three years of intensive debates among the experts of CAHAR, which finally proposed a 'Draft Agreement on Responsibility for Examining Asylum Requests' in 1989.[12] Invoking the liberal and humanitarian traditions of the member states of the Council of Europe, the agreement calls for effective co-operation in order to grant persons who are persecuted as per Article 1 of the Geneva Convention 'the full protection secured to them by the said Convention' by establishing a state responsible for examining an asylum application so as to combat the phenomenon of refugees 'in orbit'. The central provision of the draft agreement is that the state, which the asylum seeker has entered first, should be responsible for the examination of his or her asylum claim. Exceptions to this rule may be made when another party has issued a visa or residence permit to the person concerned, or if he or she has close family members in another country. However, individual states reserve the right to examine an application even where the responsibility of another state is determined. Furthermore, in order to avoid a downwards harmonisation, the draft expressly states that 'nothing in this Agreement shall be interpreted as precluding a Party from examining an asylum application on wider grounds existing in its national law or practice.'[13]

At the time this draft agreement was reached, however, CAHAR had lost its leading position in the harmonisation of European refugee policies. Instead of seeking harmonisation in the humanitarian framework of the Council of Europe, EU member states shifted co-operation to more selective intergovernmental fora. While the Council of Europe's heterogeneous composition made an agreement over this issue between the major refugee-receiving countries and traditional transit countries unlikely, two other initiatives were launched among EU member states. The Council of Europe has continued to issue declarations, reports and recommendations on refugees. In line with its humanitarian mandate, it has focused on the improvement of the standards of refugee protection in Europe and, in particular, the establishment of a common policy for *de facto* refugees not recognised under the criteria laid down in the Geneva Convention. However, these efforts have had little impact on member states' policies. Instead, a second form of co-operation has evolved which is determined by the intergovernmental negotiations amongst EU Ministers for Immigration.

INTERGOVERNMENTAL NEGOTIATIONS IN THE 1980'S

The intergovernmental co-operation amongst EU member states was inspired less by the growing pressure of the world refugee problem or the need to reform the system of international refugee protection in a common, harmonised approach than by the reaction of national governments to the forthcoming abolition of internal border controls in the context of the single market project.[14]

This reaction was linked to the affirmation of the establishment of a single market by 1992 in the Single European Act of 1986 and herewith–in addition to the liberalisation of goods, services and capital–the introduction of free movement of persons, leading to an abolition of internal border controls. The rationale behind the emerging co-operation was the perception that the abolition of border controls would lead to a loss of control over the entry of persons to the territory, thereby opening up the way for illegal immigration of undesired persons such as criminals, terrorists, and drug traffickers but also economic migrants and asylum seekers. With regard to asylum seekers, it was feared that freedom of movement would be accompanied by an increased abuse of domestic asylum procedures through the simultaneous or repetitive allocation of multiple asylum claims in several member states, or 'asylum shopping'. These fears were particularly expressed by the governments of traditional refugee receiving countries who feared that, given the relative laxity of immigration control in Southern member states, they would lose all means of controlling illegal immigration or the entry of asylum seekers to their territory.

Thus, co-operation in asylum and immigration matters emerged as a counter-reaction to the prospect of an abolition of internal borders and was presented as a necessary compensatory measure to safeguard internal stability and security. In order to counter the perceived security deficit engendered by free movement, the EU member states promoted a general strengthening of the external borders of the Union through the adoption of strict entry provisions, the intensification of border controls, and the adoption of common measures against undesired trans-national phenomena such as international crime, drug trafficking, terrorism, but also illegal immigration and demands for asylum.

The Institutional Framework

Co-operation in asylum and immigration matters evolved out-side the Community framework. In 1988 a proposal by the European Commission for a directive on the harmonisation of asylum law and the status of refugees was rejected by the member states, which invoked the lack of Community compe-tence in these central matters of national sovereignty (Lobko-wicz 1990: 97; 1993a: 12), [15] although the formulation of such a proposal was provided by the 1985 White Paper of the Euro-pean Commission on the Completion of the Internal Market.[16] Faced with this opposition, the Commission assumed a prag-matic stance and decided to leave the field to the discretion of the member states instead of getting bogged down in quarrels over sovereignty and lengthy procedures requiring the partici-pation of the European and national parliaments (Lobkowicz 1993a: 12; 1993b: 12).

Two more or less parallel intergovernmental processes be-tween European governments promoted intergovernmental co-operation in asylum and immigration matters–the 'Schengen' and the 'Ad Hoc Group Immigration'. The lead was taken by the traditional refugee receiving countries–Germany, France and the Benelux countries whose co-operation goes back to a Franco-German initiative of 1984, in which Chancellor Kohl and President Mitterrand agreed on the gradual abolition of controls at the common borders.[17] Shortly afterwards, the Benelux countries decided to join the initiative, which led to the adoption of the First Schengen Agreement on the Gradual Abolition of Checks at the Common Borders of July 1985 (Pauly 1993:

187ff.). This core of five member states willing to implement the free movement of persons as soon as possible were the pioneers of the integration process. This initiative was to become a pilot project, a sort of 'laboratory' functioning in a limited number of member states, which would serve as an example for EU-wide co-operation. In doing so, Schengen became a prototype of differentiated integration.

The negotiations between this limited group of member states led to the adoption of the Second Schengen Agreement applying the First Schengen Agreement in 1990.[18] This agreement, which was predominantly formulated by representatives of the national interior ministries, set the conditions for the abolition of border checks amongst the signatory states and the corresponding compensatory measures considered necessary to safeguard internal security. Apart from regulations on the fight against drugs, terrorism, international crime and police and judicial co-operation, compensation included measures relating to the entry and the expulsion of non-EC citizens and asylum seekers. The shift in the Schengen negotiations towards issues concerning third-state nationals is striking in so far as the First Schengen Agreement of 1985 only planned a harmonisation of visa policies and, where necessary, general measures regarding aliens' law, while the implementation agreement provided far-reaching regulations in the fields of asylum and immigration.

In contrast to the Schengen initiative, which started among a limited number of countries, co-operation between all member states in asylum and immigration matters took place in the so-called 'Ad Hoc Group Immigration' established in 1986. This group emerged from an already existing forum, the 'TREVI' group, which can be traced back to the mid-1970s.[19] TREVI was founded at the European Council in Fontainebleau in 1976 without any contractual basis and outside the Community framework. Its task was to co-ordinate home and justice affairs in the field of internal security and public order, especially in matters of terrorism and international crime. The TREVI group initially concentrated on the fight against an apprehended 'Euroterrorism', but its scope was qualitatively expanded in the mid-1980s as a reaction to the confirmation of the internal market project in the Single European Act. Fearing a loss of control over immigration into their territories after the abolition of internal borders, the TREVI ministers decided to establish a formally independent *ad hoc* group on immigration, with a remit to formulate compensatory measures in the fields of asylum and immigration to 'safeguard of internal security' (Bigo 1992: 54; Rupprecht and Hellenthal 1992: 154). In addition, a sub-group on asylum was created with a mandate to examine the measures to be taken to achieve a common policy and to put an end to the abusive use of the right to asylum (Hailbronner 1989: 21; Lobkowicz 1993a). Other sub-groups dealt with external borders, visas, exchange of information, and false documents. Even though the Ad Hoc Group was formally only a consultative forum independent from the TREVI group, it was, at least at the top personal level, identical with the latter–which emphasises the linkage between the classical threats to internal security, such as terrorism and crime, with the new 'threat' of immigration.[20] In contrast to these original subjects of concern in the TREVI group, co-operation in asylum matters evolved rapidly and led to the adoption of two intergovernmental agreements: the Dublin Convention on the State Responsible for the Examination of a Asylum Claim of 15 June 1990,[21] and the draft Convention on the Crossing of External Borders.[22] These agreements take over the respective provisions of the Second Schengen Agreement.

This convergent output of both intergovernmental forums indicates the strongly interlinked nature of the negotiations. Communication between the two groups was ensured by their parallel organisational structures and the fact that members of the Schengen group were also represented in the Ad Hoc Group Immigration. Given this overlap, and the fact that both groups operated outside the Community framework screened from public scrutiny, the Schengen states were able to transmit their proposals to the agenda of 'the Twelve' and developed into a sort of 'motor' for EU-wide co-operation. Below the ministerial level, all members, agendas, protocols or decision-making procedures were kept strictly confidential. The European Commission was allowed to observe the meetings of the Ad Hoc Group but was completely excluded from the 'Schengen' sessions until 1989, when the Second Agreement was drafted. Neither the European nor the national parliaments participated in this process; they received no regular information and were not able to exercise any control over these negotiations.[23]

The Schengen and Dublin Conventions

The two processes presented above, although starting from quite different positions, led to a common set of rules with regard to asylum seekers and the entry of third-state nationals. Whereas the Schengen process was initially designed to promote the implementation of the single market, co-operation in the Ad Hoc Group Immigration followed a defensive logic oriented towards the avoidance of security deficits following the abolition of internal border controls. The interesting point, however, is the final convergence of the two processes as regards results. It appears that the objective of free circulation was 'paid for in terms of restrictions on the subject' (O'Keeffe 1996: 2); that is, the abolition of internal borders controls was traded off against the restriction of entry to the territory and an affirmation of states' sovereignty to control immigration from outside the Community.

From a comparative point of view, the Schengen Agreement is broader than the Dublin Convention with regard to scope, but narrower in the number of participating parties. In contrast to the Dublin Convention, it deals not only with asylum seekers but also with the crossing of external borders and the harmonisation of visa policies, co-operation of police, customs and justice. Furthermore, it provides for the establishment of a computerised register of persons to be refused entry to the EU, or whose movement within the EU is to be restricted–the Schengen Information System (SIS) (Mahmood 1995). Despite these differences, both agreements correspond in their asylum provisions. The regulations regarding external borders were also widely replicated in the Draft External Borders Convention among all member states, which, however, could not be signed because of conflicts between Spain and the UK over the status of Gibraltar.

The Dublin Convention followed the Schengen example, whose preparatory works were already largely completed by 1988.[24] It is remarkable that no serious progress was achieved concerning police (Europol), customs or judicial co-operation until late 1992 (Busch 1996a: 8). The fact that agreement was first reached over the issue of asylum illustrates the priority given to this field of co-operation by the member states. This is reinforced by the Schengen Agreement, where detailed and far-reaching provisions were drawn up with regard to asylum seekers, whereas the provisions dealing with the original focal points in police and judicial co-operation or the fight against drug trafficking remain very general and are more an expression of a general desire for future co-operation than a legal basis for current operations (Nanz 1994: 101).

Several states–Portugal and Spain in June 1991, Italy in November 1991 and Greece in November 1992–joined the Schengen Agreement after it was signed. Accession was made conditional on the sealing of the external borders through intensified control mechanisms and the implementation of tighter restrictions on immigration and asylum. After several delays due to problems with the implementation of the Schengen Information System, the agreement finally came into force in March 1995 between Germany, France, the Benelux countries, Spain and Portugal. In the meantime, all member states, with the exception of the UK and Ireland, joined the Schengen initiative.[25] However, its implementation is limping. France introduced several exceptions, especially in the field of police co-operation, because of national security interests (Rijt 1997: 12). In addition, the full participation of countries such as Italy, Greece, and Austria was delayed several times on the grounds that their external borders were not sufficiently tight. With the Amsterdam Treaty of 1997, the Schengen 'acquis' was introduced into the

EU framework. The implementation of the Dublin Convention was equally fraught, but it finally came into force after the last member state had ratified it in September 1997, seven years after it was signed.

The impact of these agreements on European asylum policies has been considerable. Although initially framed as a limited side-aspect of the implementation of the single market, the two agreements redefine the rules of international co-operation in asylum matters amongst EU member states and restrict the conditions of entry for third-country nationals in general. With regard to entry, the Schengen Conventions set down strict requirements and intensified control standards. In short, any person who is not a citizen of a member state can only enter the common territory if he or she holds a valid travel document, has a valid visa where applicable, is not on the list of entry refusals, has justification for the purpose of stay or transit, and has sufficient means of subsistence (Drüke 1993: 105). Furthermore, the contracting parties agree to introduce sanctions against transport agencies who enable the entry of persons not meeting these requirements and to harmonise visa policies.

While these provisions apply to third-state nationals in general, the central rule regarding asylum is the implementation of a system of redistribution for handling asylum claims based on the 'first host country' or the 'safe third country' rule. This rule establishes the single responsibility of one signatory state for the examination of an asylum claim. The criteria which determine this responsibility follow the principle of entry authorisation. Accordingly, responsibility lies with the state which has issued a residence permit or visa to the applicant or which has enabled, with or without authorisation, his or her entry. An exception to this rule is made when the asylum seeker has close family members who have already been granted refugee status in another member state.

The agreements do not aim at substantive harmonisation as both the procedures for the examination of an asylum claim and the criteria for the determination of refugee status remain within the competence of the member states. With the rule of exclusive responsibility, however, the member states agree to respect each other's decisions on the granting or refusal of refugee status.[26] The basis of this mutual recognition is the assumption of comparable legislation in the field deriving from their common obligations under the Geneva Convention of 1951 as amended by its New York Protocol of 1967.[27] This, however, is a questionable assumption, if one bears in mind the different interpretations of this Convention illustrated in Chapter 1.

The main purpose of these measures with regard to refugees is evident: to prevent the uncontrolled movement of asylum seekers in the European Union and limit their access to member states' territories and asylum procedures. Starting from the idea that multiple requests would represent an abuse of asylum procedures or 'asylum shopping', the responsibility rule of the Schengen and Dublin Conventions prevents multiple simultaneous or successive applications by one and the same asylum seeker in different member states.

Linking up with earlier negotiations in the framework of the Council of Europe, the preamble to the Dublin Convention also sets out the goal of preventing the problem of 'refugees in orbit'. In fact, the fixing of a responsibility rule for the examination of an asylum claim has always been considered a way to avoid situations where asylum seekers travel from one country to another without finding one willing to examine their claim. However, in this case, both the mandate of the Ad Hoc Group Immigration, which focused on the abuse of asylum procedures, and the contents of the Treaty tend to undermine this aim. Considering that the main causes of the problem of 'refugees in orbit' lie in 'the legal differences between [...] States, and in the attitudes and practices of the authorities dealing with refugee matters' (Grahl-Madsen 1980: 95), a policy to resolve this would at least presuppose a harmonisation of the basic substantive and procedural provisions of national asylum laws (see Bolten 1991: 18ff.). This conclusion is supported by the fact that the prevention of orbit situations is not mentioned in the Schengen Agreement, which served as model for the Dublin text and contains the same provisions with regard to asylum seekers.

Rather, the accompanying measures, such as the strengthening of external borders, the extension of visa requirements, and the introduction of penalties for travel agencies enabling entry to persons without the necessary documents, tend to inhibit the access to asylum procedures for genuine refugees and bogus applicants alike. Moreover, if one considers the very disparate distribution of the numbers of asylum seekers among EU member states in the second half of the 1980s,[28] an additional motivation for the establishment of this system of responsibility becomes clear, that is, the redistribution of asylum seekers from the more affected to the less affected countries in the EU.

FROM MAASTRICHT TO AMSTERDAM

While the Dublin and Schengen Agreements did not set out to establish a thorough harmonisation of immigration and asylum policies, they did set demarcation lines for the future refugee regime as subsequently implemented in the EU framework. Two dynamics supported the pursuit of this co-operation in the European Union. The first is implicit in the Dublin and Schengen Agreements and their core rule, which determines the exclusive responsibility of one member state. This rule requires the interchangeability of policy decisions and thus presupposes a common standard of refugee protection and the existence of equivalent status determination criteria. As shown in Chapter 1, however, this is not the case. A second factor supporting co-operation is the evolution of the refugee problem itself and the changes occurring in the international system. In particular, the opening up of the Eastern bloc and the persistence of ethnic and political conflicts the world over generated the perception of a threatening increase of potential immigrants and asylum seekers in particular from and through the countries of Central and Eastern Europe.

Towards a 'European' Refugee Policy

The guidelines of this second phase of co-operation were laid down in a working programme issued by the Ad Hoc Group Immigration in preparation for the Maastricht Treaty.[29] Generally speaking, the subsequent Europeanisation distinguishes itself from the intergovernmental agreements through its detachment from the problem of internal border controls within the single market, and its explicit claim for a common 'European' approach to the issues of asylum and immigration. Despite this broader perspective, it clearly carried on with the same logic of action adopted in the first years of co-operation. The Maastricht programme focused on the fight against the abuse of asylum procedures. The document established a list of priorities falling into two categories, 'migration' and 'asylum'. With regard to immigration, the ministers agreed on the harmonisation of entry criteria for third-state nationals and called for measures to combat illegal immigration. In the field of asylum, the first priority was the implementation of the Dublin Convention, followed by the need to harmonise substantive matters for its implementation. Here, the ministers' primary objective was the adoption of common criteria to determine manifestly unfounded asylum applications so as to filter out bogus applicants rapidly and, as a result, to speed up domestic asylum procedures. In a second part, the ministers set out a number of measures regarded as less urgent, including the harmonisation of the interpretation of the definition of a refugee according to the Geneva Convention, and the harmonisation of expulsion policies and the establishment of a common centre for information on legal, political, juridical and statistical matters.

This working programme is a conclusive synopsis of European co-operation in immigration and asylum matters. It not only states the current stage and future aims of harmonisation, but also reflects the underlying logic through the establishment of priorities. In sum, these priorities are the prevention of abusive asylum claims and the reduction of asylum seekers on the territory of the member states.

The Third Pillar

On the basis of the working programme of the Ministers for Immigration, the issues of asylum and immigration were for the first time introduced into the framework of the Union in Title VI of the Treaty on European Union (TEU) of February 1992 as 'matters of common interest'. The list of these matters reflected the history of their salience on the European agenda. It comprised the questions of asylum, the crossing of external borders, immigration, drugs, and fraud, together with judicial, customs and police co-operation. Although now formally integrated into the structure of the European Union, co-operation in these matters was left to the intergovernmental level. This third pillar[30] of the Maastricht Treaty only provided limited institutional innovations and formalised the existing structure of the Ad Hoc Group Immigration. The Council of Ministers retained an exclusive competence to take decisions in these areas. As instruments, it could adopt joint positions and actions and draw up conventions. The European Commission was given a new right to initiative, and the European Parliament (EP) was allowed a limited involvement foreseen through its regular information and consultation on principal aspects of the activities in these areas. Even though these provisions already accorded limited powers to the supranational bodies, in practice their role was even more limited. The Commission initiatives were largely ignored, and the Parliament was not regularly informed or consulted (Fortescue 1995). The opposition of the member states to a greater involvement of the supranational bodies was also reflected in the decision not to apply the so-called 'passerelle' of Article K.9, which would have allowed the transfer of asylum and immigration matters to the supranational first pillar by a unanimous vote of the Council. Furthermore, the member states, reluctant to engage in binding obligations through the formalisation of their co-operation, opted for the adoption of informal, non-binding instruments such as 'resolutions' and 'conclusions' which were not included under the provisions of the Maastricht Treaty.

This institutional structure of co-operation under the Maastricht Treaty not only introduced important intergovernmental

elements into the EU framework, but also had important reper-
cussions on the decision-making process at the national level of
the member states and the distribution of competences between the legislature, the executive and the courts and within
the government administration. In short, the transfer of decision-making powers to the Council of Ministers at the European
level strengthened the domestic role of the members of the
Council *vis-à-vis* other ministries and *vis-à-vis* national parliaments. With regard to the division of competences within the
executive, the selective involvement of mainly members of the
respective Ministries of the Interior has weakened the role of
the Ministries of Foreign Affairs or Social Affairs in the field of
asylum and immigration in all member states. National parliaments have very little impact on European policy-making. In the
case of international conventions, the need for ratification allows parliaments to adopt a proposed text in all its parts, or,
with the risk of creating internal and international tensions, to
simply reject it.[31] With the instruments of action adopted under
the Treaty on European Union, even this last opportunity for
parliamentary control is absent. Contrary to the instruments of
'joint positions', 'joint actions' and 'international conventions'
provided in the Treaty, the Council only adopted 'soft law'
resolutions and conclusions which did not require ratification
and were usually immediately implemented by the competent
ministers. This democratic deficit is reinforced by the lack of
judicial control over these issues, as neither the European
Court of Justice nor national courts have so far had the right of
jurisdiction over these grey areas of international law.

The Amsterdam Treaty

The Maastricht Treaty setting up the European Union was conceived as a dynamic structure which would be revised on a
regular basis. By the time the first comprehensive reform of the
Treaty was started in 1996, ending the adoption of the Amster-

dam Treaty concluded in June 1997, dissatisfaction with the functioning of the third pillar was widespread and consensual (Hix and Niessen 1996). The critique focused on the lack of democratic and judicial control, the inefficiency of the instruments and decisions adopted, and the lack of conceptual clarity underlying the policies chosen.

In order to overcome these deficits, the policy fields of asylum and immigration were transferred to the supranational first pillar of the Treaty on the European Union under a new Title called 'Visas, Asylum, Immigration and other Policies related to the Free Movement of Persons'. However, significant intergovernmental elements were taken over due to the persistent opposition of several national governments to the transfer of sovereignty in these sensitive matters. As a general rule, organisational changes should only occur after a 'transitional period' of five years following the entry into force of the revised Treaty. Then, the Commission will be granted the sole right of initiative and the Council will take a decision regarding the greater involvement of the European Parliament. The central decision-making body remains the Council which, contrary to previous expectations, continues to work under the unanimity rule.

A more significant amendment was taken with regard to the role of the European Court of Justice, which is granted the competence to give preliminary and interpretative rulings over Council acts in asylum and immigration matters. However, this competence could in practice be limited by the accompanying clause that it should not apply to measures 'relating to the maintenance of law and order and the safeguarding of internal security'.[32]

Finally, another central innovation is the introduction of the Schengen 'acquis' into the EU framework. With regard to asylum, the corresponding provisions of the Schengen Agreement were rendered obsolete with the entry into force of the Dublin Convention. Its inclusion in the Treaty on European Union will nevertheless have important consequences for the control of external borders, policing and judicial co-operation.

While the implementation of the revised Treaty will show how far member states are willing to allow the full communitarisation of these core elements of national sovereignty, the numerous opt-outs to the provisions on asylum and immigration and the Schengen Protocol are indicative of the reluctance of some governments. In particular, the UK, Ireland and Denmark negotiated extensive exception clauses to co-operation in these matters, which in practice allow them to choose whether they wish to participate or not, measure by measure.

More substantively, a heavily disputed innovation was the successful Spanish proposal to exclude EU citizens from the right of asylum in the EU, thereby introducing a *de facto* geographical limitation to the Geneva Convention, the underlying intention being to prevent, among other things, members of the separatist Basque organisation ETA from being granted asylum in another member state as had been the case in France and Belgium. While it is not yet clear whether this Protocol will really affect the policies of member states, it illustrates the controversial political and diplomatic character of the act of conceding asylum.

The 'Acquis'

Co-operation under the Maastricht Treaty followed the guidelines established in the working programme of the Ministers for Immigration of 1991 only in part. In contrast to the emphasis placed on the need to harmonise substantive aspects of refugee law in the programme, the Ministers for Immigration concentrated their co-operation on the implementation of the Dublin Convention and the adoption of restrictive measures in the fight against bogus asylum applications. Compared to the earlier modes of action in the Schengen and the Ad Hoc Group Immigration, the instruments of the Maastricht Treaty allowed much speedier procedures. Whereas negotiations on the Schengen and Dublin Conventions lasted five years before they were signed and another five to seven years to come into–partial–force, several resolutions and conclusions have been adopted and implemented since 1992.[33] The speed with which these measures were approved is due to the fact that they are informal in nature and not legally binding, thus leaving the discretion over implementation to the competent minister and avoiding the sometimes lengthy procedure of ratification in the national parliaments. Furthermore, the vast majority of these measures did not deal with the more controversial questions of material or procedural refugee law but aimed instead at the implementation of the Dublin Convention and at the adoption of simplified procedures for 'manifestly unfounded' asylum claims.

The initial dynamism of co-operation corresponded to the Declaration of the Ministers for Immigration annexed to the Treaty on the European Union, where they gave priority to questions concerning asylum policies in their co-operation under the third pillar. Accordingly, progress in the field of immigration has been less incisive, with only limited resolutions being adopted with regard to labour immigration[34] and illegal employment.[35] A resolution was also adopted regarding the harmonisation of national policies on family reunification which may also apply to many refugees who have obtained a legal status other than that of a refugee under the Geneva Convention.[36]

THE CLEARING HOUSE

As a first step in the fulfilment of the working programme of the Ad Hoc Group was the creation of a Clearing House (CIREA)[37] to gather and exchange information on asylum seekers in 1992. This measure was taken in order to implement Article 14 of the Dublin Convention, which provides for the obligatory mutual exchange of information on relevant aspects of asylum policies. The Clearing House is an informal forum composed of asylum policy officials from the member states, and with the full association of the European Commission. The information compiled covers data on member states' legislation and practice in the field of asylum policy, statistics on arrivals of asylum seekers, important case law and legal principles in the member states and the European Court of Human Rights in Strasbourg, and assessments of the situation in the countries of origin or provenance of the asylum seekers. These assessments have so far been prepared within the framework of the Common Foreign and Security Policy (CFSP), based on reports by the diplomatic missions of the member states which are then agreed after consultation with the Ministries of Foreign Affairs of the member states. They serve as the basis for decisions in individual asylum cases and for the implementation of the 'safe third country' and 'safe country of origin' policies. The fact that the assessments are formulated within this diplomatic framework, which is, by definition, closed and secretive, has been much criticised (see, for example, Amnesty International 1993). As a reaction, a closer co-operation with the information base of the UNHCR in Geneva is currently under consideration.[38]

THE LONDON RESOLUTION ON MANIFESTLY UNFOUNDED APPLICATIONS FOR ASYLUM

The resolution on manifestly unfounded applications for asylum is one of three measures decided at the meeting of the Ad Hoc Group Immigration in London on 30 November–1 December 1992 aiming at the adoption of efficient procedures in the fight against bogus asylum seekers. This resolution states that applications for asylum shall be considered as manifestly unfounded when 'there is clearly no substance to the applicant's claim to fear persecution in his own country' or when 'the claim is based on deliberate deception or is an abuse of asylum procedures'. The first applies to cases where there is no indication of persecution, for example, when the applicant only cites economic reasons for his or her application, but also when it is deemed that the applicant would be safe in another area of the country. It also covers cases where the applicant is from a country where there is generally no serious risk of persecution.

The second group of unfounded claims covers the cases of false identity or forged documents and where the applicant gives false information or refuses to co-operate. It also applies to cases where an application is submitted to forestall expulsion measures and when other applications have been submitted by the same person in other states.

These applications are processed in accelerated procedures which do not provide the full range of legal remedies. In particular, the time-limits for requests and appeals and the opportunities for appeal are all limited, and there is little access to legal advisors or NGOs. Some safeguards were finally added to the resolution after an earlier draft had become public and triggered a wave of protest. These include the chance to take into account information received from the UNHCR, as well as some procedural guarantees, such as the opportunity of a personal interview with a qualified official or simplified review procedures. Furthermore, the burden on the applicant to provide 'evidence' about the well-foundedness of his or her case was replaced by the obligation to provide 'indications'. A last important amendment to the draft was the introduction of a specific reference to the UNHCR and the Geneva Convention in the Preamble. When reflecting on the motivation for this resolution, one should consider that the original text of the Preamble expressed the wish to exclude asylum-seekers in general by stating that 'those who fear violations of their human rights should if possible remain in their own countries and seek protection or redress from their own authorities or under regional human rights instruments'.[39]

THE LONDON RESOLUTION ON A HARMONISED APPROACH TO QUESTIONS CONCERNING 'SAFE THIRD COUNTRIES'

The resolution on 'safe third countries' was the second adopted in London on 30 November–1 December 1992. In contrast to the Resolution on Manifestly Unfounded Applications for Asylum, which was designed to prevent abusive applications through the reduction of procedural guarantees for individual cases not meeting certain criteria, this document applies to all asylum seekers wishing to submit an application in a member state, irrespective of whether they may be regarded as refugees. In principle, this resolution takes up the system of responsibility determination contained in the Schengen and the Dublin Conventions, which is based on the rationale that an asylum claim shall be examined by the first country with which the applicant has had contact.[40] As a consequence, a state faced with an asylum claim may decide not to examine the application and to send the applicant back to a state which fulfils the criteria of 'first contact'. The principle is that the formal identification of a safe third country precedes the substantive examination of the application for asylum and its justification. In contrast to the Schengen and Dublin Agreements, the present resolution extends this system of redistribution to all potentially safe third countries. As will be shown in Chapter 3, this instrument has an incisive impact in particular on the countries of Central and Eastern Europe, which have been designated as 'safe' by numerous member states. Coupled with the subsequent conclusion of readmission agreements, the application of the 'safe third country' rule to Central and Eastern Europe has led to the unilateral incorporation of these newly liberalised countries into the emergent EU refugee regime without their having participated in the negotiations which led to the adoption of these measures. This means an extension of the system of negative redistribution for handling asylum claims among EU member states, which, given the geographical location of the CEECs at the land-borders of the Union, will mean their increasing involvement in refugee policies as gatekeepers for asylum seekers and immigrants heading for Western Europe.

The criteria for the determination of such countries is first the verification that the applicant has already found protection there or had an opportunity to apply for asylum. To this end, the mere contact with the territory is sufficient regardless of the duration of stay, also when only in transit. A country is deemed safe when the applicant should not fear for his or her life or freedom within the meaning of Article 33 of the Geneva Convention; when the applicant is not exposed to torture or inhuman or degrading treatment;[41] and when the applicant is afforded effective protection against refoulement within the meaning of the Geneva Convention. In much the same way as the Resolution on Unfounded Applications for Asylum, a reference to the relevant conclusions of the UNHCR was only introduced in the final text.

The resolution also establishes the relationship between the application of the 'safe third country' rule and the Dublin Convention and thus integrates it into the emergent system of cooperation among the member states. As a general rule, the determination of the existence of a safe third country precedes the decision on whether to transfer responsibility for examining the application to another member state pursuant to the Dublin Convention. Even if a member state is considered responsible under the criteria of the Convention, it retains the right to send the applicant to the third country. Thus, the externalisation of asylum seekers outside the European Union prevails over an internal allocation of responsibility.

From a political perspective, it is important to note that, in contrast to the system of redistribution established within the EU, this rule has been negotiated unilaterally without the participation of the third states concerned. Having been formulated exclusively from the perspective of the sending countries, it neutralises the question of responsibility, as it does not stipulate the conditions of readmission and the duty to grant access to asylum procedure for the third country in question. Given that international law derives a responsibility of readmission only for states' own citizens, there is no legal basis for these states to agree to take back a third-state national. Furthermore, the resolution does not take into consideration the specific needs of an asylum seeker as compared to an illegal immigrant when being returned; that is, the specification of the need to provide access to fair and equitable asylum procedures in order to avoid refoulement. Given the fact that many of these 'safe countries' had not participated in the international refugee regime before, they are only now starting to implement specific asylum regulations (see Chapter 3).

THE LONDON CONCLUSIONS ON COUNTRIES WHERE THERE IS GENERALLY NO SERIOUS RISK OF PERSECUTION

These conclusions are connected to the Resolution on Manifestly Unfounded Applications and were adopted at the same meeting of the Ministers Responsible for Immigration in London. Their goal is to establish criteria whereby as a general rule a country may be characterised as 'safe' and accordingly should not produce refugees. While in earlier drafts these countries were referred to as 'safe countries of origin', the negotiators replaced the term, which was considered potentially misleading, and the final text defines them as countries 'which can be clearly shown, in an objective and verifiable way, normally not to generate refugees or where it can be clearly shown, in an objective and verifiable way, that circumstances which might in the past have justified recourse to the 1951 Geneva Convention have ceased to exist'. Elements taken into consideration for such an assessment are past numbers of refugees and recognition rates, the observance of human rights both formally and in practice, the existence of democratic institutions, and the stability of all these elements. While the original intention was to draw up a common list of such countries, the final decision was to establish general guidelines to be followed by the member states when assessing the situation in the countries of origin. The reason for this was the fear that the publication of such a list might lead to diplomatic tensions with countries of origin which would immediately be stigmatised as 'refugee producing' if not included.

The notion of countries in which there is generally no serious risk of persecution is designed to accelerate procedures which follow the guidelines set down in the Resolution on Manifestly Unfounded Applications for Asylum. Generally, the assessment by a member state of a country as 'safe' should not lead to the automatic refusal of all applications from its nationals. However, the burden of proof lies with the applicant, who has to rebut the presumption that he or she did not fear persecution in that country.

The formulation of these conclusions was controversial and is reflected in the choice of the term 'conclusions' rather than the more assertive expression 'resolution'. In much the same way as the two London resolutions, the drafts were initially much more restrictive. In the last instance, the establishment of a common list was rejected, and the term 'safe country' was dropped in favour of the more complicated expression 'countries in which there is generally no serious risk of persecution'. Furthermore, regarding the establishment of criteria to assess the safety of a country, the negotiators recognised that an overemphasis on low recognition rates might lead to a lack of flexibility with regard to changing circumstances in the country. In contrast, the role of the UNHCR was reduced in the final version. As a reaction to the UNHCR's veto on the contents of the conclusions, the desire to include its information in the assessment process on a regular basis was replaced by the agreement to accord it a 'specific place'.

In sum, the London Resolutions and Conclusions aim to reduce pressure on national asylum determination systems by two strategies: the rapid singling out of applications which are regarded as bogus, and the externalisation of those asylum seekers who do not reach the Union's territory directly but who have passed through a country in which they could have found protection. With the 'safe third country' rule, the system of redistributing responsibility for handling asylum claims is extended from the circle of the EU member states to potentially all third countries which fulfil the requirements. Geographically speaking, this mainly affects the neighbouring countries of the Union, in particular at its eastern borders.

PROCEDURAL GUARANTEES FOR THE TREATMENT OF ASYLUM SEEKERS

In their report to the European Council meeting in Maastricht,[42] the Ministers for Immigration agreed that the ultimate effect of the Schengen and Dublin Conventions was much greater than originally anticipated. They realised that the functioning of the conventions implicitly presupposed that member states had confidence in each other's asylum policies and hence required the harmonisation of basic procedural and substantive legal rules. However, co-operation continued to focus on the fight against bogus applications and other means to limit the intake of asylum seekers. It was only in the mid-1990s that member states were able to reach an agreement on certain legal safeguards and a common interpretation of the very basis of refugee law, that is, the criteria which determine who is a refugee.

Under the pressure from the UNHCR and other humanitarian agencies, the Ministers for Immigration finally agreed on a Resolution for Minimum Guarantees for Asylum Procedures in June 1995. These guarantees cover the rights of asylum seekers during the procedure of examination, appeal and revision of their application, manifestly unfounded asylum requests at the border and the rights of non-accompanied minors and women. In sum, the ministers have agreed on the lowest common denominator.

Critics of these guarantees focus on two aspects. First, they observe that, since it is not legally binding, the resolution cannot provide guarantees for individuals, and secondly they note the fact that it contains numerous exceptions which tend to weaken the effectiveness of the guarantees. This is particularly applicable to the exceptions made on the suspensive effect of an appeal and the lack of precise safeguards for the application of the 'safe third country' rule, particularly with regard to the obligation to ensure that the applicant will actually be given access to fair and equitable asylum procedures in the third country. In the absence of such an agreement between the sending and the receiving authorities, the application of the above-mentioned resolution may well create orbit situations or chain deportations (ECRE and Amnesty International 1995; UNHCR 1995b).

HARMONISING THE DEFINITION OF 'REFUGEE'

The first step towards the adoption of a common refugee definition and which helped decipher the commonalities and differences regarding the interpretation of the definition of the

Geneva Convention took the form of a questionnaire distributed to the member states in July 1990 (Spijkerboer 1993: Annex I). The response to the questionnaire represented the starting point for harmonisation. Although the survey was completed in 1991 (Plender 1995: 155), the adoption of common guidelines of interpretation was only given priority by the German Presidency in summer 1994. Since this aim touches the very foundations of refugee law, negotiations proved to be very tenacious. After two more years of discussion, the ministers finally agreed on a joint position in 1996 which,[43] like the Resolution on Minimum Guarantees, reflects the lowest common denominator of member-state practices. This document sets out guidelines for the application of criteria for recognition and admission as a refugee. It refers to the establishment of evidence required for granting refugee status; defines the term 'persecution' within the meaning of Article 1A of the Geneva Convention and enumerates the grounds of persecution; clarifies the conditions in which civil war and other internal or generalised armed conflicts can be causes of persecution; discusses the relocation within the country of origin as well as the issue of refugees 'sur place';[44] clarifies the issues of conscientious objection, absence without leave and desertion as grounds for persecution; and finally, addresses the cessation of refugee status.

These guidelines are in sharp contrast to today's main causes of refugee flows and illustrate the refusal to adapt the definition of a refugee to changed circumstances. In particular, they limit the application of refugee protection to persons who are persecuted by the state, either directly or with its tolerance or complicity. The person who is persecuted by a third party and who the state is unable to protect does not come within this definition. Thus, it disqualifies the majority of today's refugees from refugee status according to the Geneva Convention, namely those escaping from civil war and generalised violence. This limitation of the applicability of the Geneva Convention contrasts with the more liberal stance followed until recently by several member states.[45]

ACTIONS TAKEN WITH REGARD TO REFUGEES FROM THE FORMER YUGOSLAVIA

The EU's reaction to the refugee drama in the former Yugoslavia is ambivalent. On the one hand, innovative measures were developed which introduced a new set of concepts and strategies in European asylum policies. On the other hand, the failure to reach an equitable distribution of refugees among the member states reflects not only the unwillingness to take in additional refugees, but also the lack of solidarity within the Union.

Refugees from the former Yugoslavia are a typical case of *de facto* refugees who are generally not subsumed under the definition of the Geneva Convention but who are accepted on humanitarian grounds. European countries have usually offered protection to such persons on a relatively unformalised, *ad hoc* basis, which differs markedly from state to state. In the case of Yugoslavia, we observe first signs of a possible systematisation and formalisation of *de facto* policies under the label of 'temporary protection'.

European Union action in this field was inspired by German concerns to obtain some sort of burden-sharing in the matter, in particular during its EU presidency from July to December 1994. Germany, which accepted by far the greatest share of Balkan refugees in Europe,[46] found additional support for its claim from the Council of Europe and UNHCR, which, from a humanitarian point of view, have always sought to promote solidarity and cooperation among receiving countries (Thorburn 1995: 475–76).

A first Conclusion on People Displaced by the Conflict in the Former Yugoslavia was adopted on 30 November 1992 in London, followed by a Resolution on Certain Guidelines as Regards the Admission of Particularly Vulnerable Groups of Persons from the Former Yugoslavia in 1993.[47] A first step in the debate on the formulation of a solidaristic system of temporary protection for refugees who did not generally satisfy the criteria laid down in the Geneva Convention amongst European states[48] was the Resolution on Burden-sharing with Regard to the Admission and Residence on a Temporary Basis of Displaced Persons, adopted by the European Council in June 1995. This resolution establishes a new system of redistribution inside the EU by taking into account prior contributions made by member states in the prevention or resolution of the crisis, the humanitarian aid provided, and factors which affect their capacity for reception. Nevertheless, it seems that the implementation of this system of burden-sharing differs highly among the member states. Not only is the distribution of refugees from the former Yugoslavia still very disparate, but the question of their return after the period of temporary protection expires has not yet been resolved.

From a broader perspective, this internal system of redistribution is only one instrument in the approach developed with regard to the crisis in the former Yugoslavia. Since the overwhelming majority of victims remained in their region of origin, international attention focused on the ex-Yugoslav territory itself, whereas the burden of refugee relief remained mainly in the hands of the UNHCR and NGOs. Two strategies have been developed which precede flight from the country. The first is the 'internalisation' of the problem, that is, the maintenance of civil war victims within their area of origin in so-called 'safe havens', more or less protected by the international community.[49] And secondly, where internalisation is not possible, there is a strategy of 'containment', that is, the attempt to regionalise the protection of refugees within the broader area of their country of origin. Taken together, these strategies indicate some degree of progress in the distribution of refugees within the Union, but only as a second alternative after an attempt has been made to limit their arrival by providing protection 'sur place'. As a consequence, the major actors in this scenario are no longer the receiving states, but the UNHCR, other international organisations and NGOs.

The Supranational Voice

According to the description of the institutional structure of co-operation in matters of asylum and immigration under the Maastricht Treaty, the European Parliament and the European

Commission have no competence to pass their own measures in the field. The member states, eager to safeguard their sovereignty over these sensitive matters, have opposed any direct influence by supranational bodies. This opposition is amplified by the fact that the positions of these two institutions contrast sharply with the restrictive orientation and secretive mode of action prevailing in the intergovernmental structure. In what follows, the main texts adopted by the European Parliament and the European Commission in the field of asylum policy are discussed. Although of little current impact, these positions may become increasingly important with a revaluation of the role of the supranational bodies in the aftermath of the Amsterdam decisions, and eventually lead to a re-orientation of European refugee policies.

INITIATIVES TAKEN BY THE EUROPEAN PARLIAMENT

The European Parliament has always pursued a very generous and liberal stance in matters relating to asylum policy. In contrast to the work of the Schengen and the *ad hoc* intergovernmental groups, its first key document, the 'Vetter Report' on the right of asylum of 1987 (EP 1987) did not start from the problem of the abolition of internal border controls and the subsequent deficits for the internal security of the single market, but from the complex causes of today's refugee problem. It called for a more generous attitude towards asylum seekers on the part of the member states, based on the commitment to universal human rights and human dignity. In particular, the report maintained that the access of asylum seekers to the member states should be preserved and condemned restrictive visa policies. Furthermore, the member states were requested to adopt a common set of legal and social minimal standards for asylum procedures, and to establish an equitable system of burden sharing with the chance to distribute financial resources from the EC budget. The document also raised questions of substantive asylum law. Starting from the analysis of today's causes and structures of refugee flows, MEPs called for the introduction of a formal legal status for *de facto* refugees and the extension of the definition of a refugee following the example of the Organisation of African Unity (see Chapter 1).

On the basis of this report, the European Parliament adopted two resolutions in March and June 1987.[50] In the second and more important of these resolutions, it sharply condemned the asylum policies of some member states as being contrary to human rights. It also criticised the intergovernmental mode of co-operation over these issues, which, bypassing both the European and national parliaments, violated the basic principles of democracy. Instead, it called for the transfer of the policy field to the competence of the European Community.

Shortly before the adoption of the Treaty on the European Union, the European Parliament again expressed its scepticism in a Resolution on harmonising asylum issues of November 1992.[51] This document re-emphasised the humanitarian dimension of asylum law and stressed the need for the member states to set an example in safeguarding human rights and human dignity. The member states were reminded of their responsibility in the matter deriving not only from their colonial past, but also from the contemporary foreign and international economic policies contributing to the global refugee problem. Furthermore, the resolution reiterated the claims of the Vetter Report and called for a comprehensive strategy, which would include the fight against the root causes of refugee movements through economic and political co-operation with the countries of origin. This line of argument was continued in the report on the general guidelines of a European refugee policy in December 1993.[52] Here, the moral, humanitarian, and historical obligations of the EU, as one of the richest regions in the world, for the protection of refugees was emphasised, as was the need to extend the refugee definition in line with that of the Organisation of African Unity.

INITIATIVES TAKEN BY THE EUROPEAN COMMISSION

The original attempt by the European Commission to develop a competence in the field of asylum and immigration following the White Paper on the internal market ran counter to the will of the member states who refused a transfer of sovereignty in these sensitive areas. The 1988 Commission proposal for a directive to stimulate the genuine harmonisation of asylum policies was rejected.[53] Contrary to the work of the intergovernmental groups, it was not based on the perception of security deficits subsequent to the establishment of the internal market but, similar to the initiatives of the European Parliament, proposed a co-operative response to a common challenge and a substantive harmonisation of the criteria determining refugee status. On this basis, it proposed a system of redistribution for handling asylum claims, which was closer to the 1988 CAHAR proposal than to the provisions of the Schengen and Dublin Agreements. In the face of opposition from the member states, the Commission preferred to leave the initiative in these matters in their hands. The strategy adopted can be described as a 'gradualist' as opposed to a 'doctrinaire' approach. It renounces bringing issues under Community competence and thus ensuring the Commission's power, and rather promotes co-operation amongst the member states in substantive terms with the expectation of an incremental shift of the institutional structures towards communitarisation (Myers 1995). In the words of Commissioner Bangemann, in the late 1980s the Commission opted for 'making progress rather than fighting time consuming battles for competence' (quoted in Myers 1995: 282).

Accordingly, the Commission has to date limited its attempts to influence co-operation in asylum and immigration matters and, assuming that progressive co-operation would automatically lead to its greater involvement, did not oppose the introduction of intergovernmental structures under the third pillar of the Maastricht Treaty. Its cautious stance is also reflected in a Communication to the Council and the European Parliament issued prior to the Maastricht Treaty in October 1991,[54] where the Commission basically approved the working programme prepared by the Ad Hoc Group Immigration. Noting the increased political and social importance of asylum policies in Europe, the document acknowledges the progress made with the Dublin Convention and emphasises additional steps to be taken in particular with regard to a more thorough harmonisation of procedural and material asylum law.

This discrete attitude reduced the anxiety of the member states regarding a possible loss of authority over matters of national sovereignty whilst simultaneously allowing the adoption of a dynamic provision in the Maastricht Treaty which anticipated the possible transfer of these policy fields to the first pillar (Art. K.9). Responding to the priority given to the field of asylum in the Treaty,[55] the Commission evaluated the prospect of applying this so-called 'passerelle' at the end of 1993, but realising that the member states were still reluctant to its greater involvement, concluded that it was not yet time for such a transfer of competence.[56]

The most complete text adopted by the European Commission in these matters is its Communication to the Council and the European Parliament of February 1994.[57] With this document, the Commission asserted its position and proposed a comprehensive strategy to deal with the global dimension of migration in a long-term perspective. In contrast to earlier proposals, this communication integrated the issues of immigration and asylum in a joint approach as closely interdependent and interconnected problems. The comprehensive approach is reminiscent of earlier proposals made by the European Parliament and addresses three problems: the root causes of migration via a common foreign policy; the management of migration flows via both immigration rules and provisions for the protection of refugees; and the long-term integration of legal immigrants in the host societies. This new strategy should be accompanied by an open discussion and an active policy of information. In this communication, the Commission criticised the intergovernmental approach to the problem and its secretive mode of operation and condemned the London Resolutions of

1992 for not providing sufficient procedural safeguards for asylum seekers by establishing pre-screening procedures which carried the risk of violating the principle of non-refoulement.[58]

While the influence of the European Commission on member states' asylum policies has remained weak, two developments may favour the evolution of its autonomous competence in the matter. Firstly, the decisions of the Amsterdam summit provide for the introduction of the right of initiative for the European Commission five years after the entry into force of the revised Treaty, which may, of course, be subject to lengthy delays. Secondly, there is the role of the Commission and its competence in questions relating to a future enlargement of the Union. The integration of the associated countries of Central and Eastern Europe into the emergent EU refugee regime has recently become an official part of the pre-adhesion strategy in preparing for EU membership. Since the enlargement of this 'acquis' is promoted by all instruments of the pre-adhesion strategy, the Commission is currently significantly expanding its influence in these policy fields.

CONCLUSION

In retracing the origins of co-operation between EU member states in asylum matters and highlighting the supporting dynamics which led to the development of an emerging EU refugee regime, we have seen that this new level of international co-operation is distinct from the principles, norms, rules, and decision-making procedures incorporated in the international refugee regime and that it redefines the role of the sovereign nation states in this policy area.

The institutional structure of the emergent EU refugee regime is a legacy of its intergovernmental genesis. Little change has occurred since European co-operation began in the Schengen Agreement and Ad Hoc Group Immigration—more substantive reforms may follow from the implementation of the Amsterdam Treaty.

To date, the main actors in this co-operation are experts from the national Ministries of the Interior. For over a decade, these actors have negotiated largely hidden from public scrutiny. Neither the supranational EU institutions–the European Commission and the European Parliament–nor the national parliaments participated in these negotiations. While the Schengen and Dublin Agreements did at least require ratification by the national parliaments, the formally non-binding resolutions and conclusions adopted under the third pillar of the TEU could be directly implemented in national legislation. Thus, at the European and national levels, the legislative power over asylum issues has shifted to the national executives. This lack of democratic control was supplemented by the complete lack of judicial control in so far as neither the European Court of Justice nor national courts have had jurisdictional power over intergovernmental instruments.

With this closed institutional configuration, the EU refugee regime evolved outside the existing structures of the international refugee regime and excluded traditional actors dealing with international protection such as the UNHCR, the Council of Europe and NGOs from participating. This exclusive institutional structure was accompanied by a closure of the circle of deliberation, which favoured the adoption of a homogeneous and limited, technical view of the refugee problem. Restricting the perspective on the border-crossing quality of asylum seekers in the internal market, this view supported the depoliticisation of a highly controversial and normative question and concentrated attention on the possible destabilising effects of liberal policies. Having been linked from the beginning with other, negative phenomena such as international crime, drug trafficking, and terrorism as a threat to internal security in the single market without internal borders, this perspective has supported the reinterpretation of refugee policies from a formerly humanitarian question to one of internal and international security (Lavenex forthcoming).

This approach to the refugee issue is reflected in the legal 'acquis' reached in this field, which basically consists of those measures considered necessary to safeguard internal security in the single market. With regard to refugees, the central purpose of this co-operation was the easing of domestic asylum procedures through two groups of measures: firstly, the fight against illegal immigration and the reduction of the numbers of asylum seekers through the limitation of access to the territory, and secondly the establishment of a system of redistribution of asylum seekers amongst the member states. With regard to the first point, the 'acquis' includes the strengthening of the external border of the Union, the intensification of control, the adoption of strict entry requirements and the introduction of extensive visa policies. The second group of measures combines a redistribution of asylum seekers inside the Union with the prevention of the abuse of domestic asylum procedures through 'asylum shopping', that is, the submission of several applications by one and the same person in different member states, by fixing the responsibility of one country for the examination of an asylum claim. This system of responsibility is based on the notion of 'first country of asylum' or 'safe third country'. Considering that this rule attributes responsibility to the state first entered by the applicant, it automatically leads to a redistribution of asylum seekers among member states to the advantage of traditional asylum countries such as Germany or France, and to a rapid transformation of former transit or emigration countries in Southern Europe into countries of immigration.

Under the Maastricht Treaty, the most important innovation was the extension of this system of redistribution inside the Union to potentially all countries outside the Union which, on account of their commitment to the Geneva Convention and the European Convention on Human Rights and Fundamental Freedoms, are deemed able to provide effective protection for refugees. Whereas the notion of 'safe third country' is not completely new in the asylum practice of Western European states, two features of the respective London Resolution are particularly salient. The first relates to the fact that since the application of the 'safe third country' rule precedes the determination of the responsibility of an EU country for the examination of an asylum claim under the Dublin Convention, it is likely to lead to a disproportionate involvement of non-EU countries in dealing with refugees heading West. The second point exacerbates the first in so far as the 'safe third country' rule also applies to cases where the asylum seeker has merely been in transit in the third country. These two crucial provisions amplify the redistributive effects of the emergent EU refugee regime and reveal its central driving force: the prevention of large numbers of applications for asylum in the European Union.

This protectionist, as opposed to co-operative, logic is also reflected in the implementation of the Schengen and Dublin Conventions in the member states. While the original aim of the agreements, the abolition of internal border controls, is still not in place, the agreements supported, and in some cases, provoked significant restrictions on domestic asylum and immigration regulations. In France and Germany, two countries with a strong tradition of refugee protection, the ratification of the Schengen Agreement was linked to a restrictive reform of constitutional asylum rights. These restrictions were presented as necessary for establishing a common European approach and implementing the system of redistribution based on the 'safe third country' rule. In short, the agreements produced what may be described as restrictive 'regulatory competition', in which each state seeks to limit its responsibilities by tightening up its external borders, the restriction of entry, and the downgrading of social and legal provisions for asylum seekers, giving rise to a 'downward harmonisation'.

In contrast to these incisive domestic developments, the implementation of the redistributive rule of the agreements is lagging behind. Many member states refuse to recognise their responsibility for the examination of asylum claims under the Dublin or Schengen Conventions and do not readmit applicants when requested to do so by another country (see, for example, German Ministry of the Interior 1996). The reasons invoked are usually a perceived lack of proof from the requesting party. This reluctant attitude to co-operation, burden-sharing and, in the last instance, losses of sovereignty is also reflected in the opposition to a common approach for the protection of *de facto* refugees such as, for example, in the case of refugees from the former Yugoslavia.

In sum, experts and observers agree that contrary to real harmonisation, 'co-operation in the fields of justice and home affairs has been desperately weak' (Cullen 1995: 65), and that after the enforcement of restrictive domestic reforms, intergovernmental co-operation 'seems to have lost sight of its very objective' (Cullen 1995: 66). Instead, the focus of attention has shifted to the neighbouring countries of Central and Eastern Europe, which are increasingly being incorporated into this emergent pan-European refugee regime.

NOTES

1. In this book, the term 'European Union' refers both to the present structure of cooperation in the European Union and to the earlier 'European Communities'.

2. The Council of Europe is an intergovernmental organisation established in 1949 whose principal aims are to protect and strengthen pluralist democracy and human rights, to seek solutions to problems facing society, and to promote the emergence of a genuine European cultural identity. As of September 1997, it has forty member states.

3. The new Central and Eastern European member states are Albania as of 13 July 1995, Bulgaria as of 7 February 1992, Croatia as of 6 November 1996, the Czech Republic as of 30 June 1993, Estonia as of 14 May 1993, the former Yugoslav Republic of Macedonia as of 9 November 1995, Hungary as of 6 November 1990, Latvia as of 10 February 1995, Lithuania as of 14 May 1993, Moldova as of 13 July 1995, Poland as of 29 November 1991, Romania as of 7 October 1993, the Slovak Republic as of 30 June 1993, Slovenia as of 14 May 1993, Ukraine as of 9 November 1995, and Russia as of 28 February 1996.

4. Council of Europe, Committee of Ministers Resolution (67)14 on asylum to persons in danger of persecution of 29 June 1967, printed in Grahl-Madsen (1980: 160–61).

5. Council of Europe, Parliamentary Assembly, Recommendation 787 (1976) on harmonisation of eligibility practice under the 1951 Geneva Convention on the Status of Refugees and the 1967 Protocol of 26 January 1976.

6. Council of Europe, Parliamentary Assembly, Recommendation 773 (1976) relating to the situation of *de facto* refugees of 26 January 1976.

7. Council of Europe, Committee of Ministers, Declaration on Territorial Asylum of 28 November 1977.

8. Council of Europe, Committee of Ministers Recommendation R(81)16 on the harmonisation of national procedures relating to asylum of 5 November 1981.

9. Council of Europe, Parliamentary Assembly, Recommendation 1016 (1985) on the living and working conditions of refugees and asylum seekers of 26 September 1985.

10. According to Loescher, transit states (in particular Italy and Austria) feared that the establishment of a responsibility rule would lead to a shift of the 'burden' of asylum seekers to their territory (Loescher 1996: 628).

11. At that time, Italy and Turkey still applied the geographical limitation of the Geneva Convention of 1951 to European countries.

12. Ad Hoc Committee of Experts on the Legal Aspects of Territorial Asylum, Refugees and Stateless Persons (CAHAR), Draft Agreement on responsibility for examining asylum requests, version of 29 November 1989, printed in Hailbronner (1989: 228–32).

13. Article 11 Draft Agreement on responsibility for examining asylum requests, version of 29 November 1989.

14. The EU Ministers Responsible for Immigration, 'Report to the Council', Annex B, 12; see also Lobkowicz (1990: 93–94).

15. COM(1988) 640.

16. COM(85) 310 final.

17. The Saarbrücken Agreement of 13 July 1984.

18. Adopted on 19 June 1990, printed in Cruz (1993: 4). Both agreements are subsequently referred to as 'the Schengen Agreement'.

19. The original meaning of the acronym 'TREVI' is contested. While some scholars maintain that it is an abbreviation for the words 'Terrorism, Radicalism, Extremism, Violence, International', others associate it with the Trevi Fountain in Rome, where the first meeting of the group was held (Cruz 1993: 18).

20. The strong links between TREVI and the Ad Hoc Group Immigration are acknowledged in a decision of the European Parliament, where the latter is simply referred to as the 'TREVI group'; European Parliament Document B2-512/87 of 18 June 1987.

21. Hereinafter referred to as 'the Dublin Convention' (*EC Bulletin* 1990(6), 165–72) .

22. Although decided in 1990, the signature of this convention had to be postponed due to disputes between the United Kingdom and Spain over the status of Gibraltar.

23. See the initiatives of the European Parliament below.

24. See Draft Schengen Agreement of September 1988 printed in Hailbronner (1989: 214ff.).

25. These countries oppose participation on the grounds of their special geographical situation, which does not allow the application of border controls as regulated in the Schengen Agreement.

26. An exception clause is provided in the treaties which upholds the right of the member states to examine a request even in cases where they are not determined responsible.

27. This is confirmed in Article 28 Schengen Convention and the Preamble of the Dublin Convention.

28. For example, in 1986, Germany had 99,700 asylum seekers, France 23,400, Italy 6,500 and the UK 5,700. In 1989, the numbers were 121,000 for Germany, 60,000 for France, 2,200 for Italy 2,200 and 16,800 for the UK (Intergovernmental Consultations 1995: 299).

29. The final document is the Report from the Ministers Responsible for Immigration to the European Council meeting in Maastricht on immigration and asylum policy, Brussels, 3 December 1991 (SN 4038/91, WGI 930).

30. This term refers to the three-tiered division of the Maastricht Treaty on the European Union of 7 February 1992 in a supranational first pillar which basically unifies the former Treaties on the European Communities, and two intergovernmental pillars: the second pillar on Common Foreign and Security Policy and the third pillar on Justice and Home Affairs.

31. This condition has faced quite some opposition from the national parliaments at the moment of ratification of the Schengen and Dublin Conventions. For example in France, the deputies were informed about the contents of the Schengen Agreement only three weeks before ratification, see Santel (1995: 191). According to Cruz, no parliamentary questioning ever took place in Germany, France, Belgium and Luxembourg between 1985 and 1989. Only the Dutch Parliament was more or less regularly informed by its government (Cruz 1993: 6).

32. Article 68 II Treaty on the European Union (consolidated version of the Amsterdam revisions).

33. In contrast to the instruments laid down in Art. K.3.2 of the Treaty on the European Union (joint positions and actions as well as conventions) the Ministers Responsible for Immigration have preferred to draw up resolutions and conclusions which are the instruments of action foreseen in the field of Common Foreign and Security Policy.

34. Council Resolution of 20 June 1994 on limitations on the admission of third-country nationals to the territory of the member states for employment; Council Resolution of 30 November 1994 relating to the limitations on the admission of third-country nationals to the territory of the member states for the purpose of pursuing activities as self-employed persons; and Council

Resolution of 30 November 1994 on the admission of third-country nationals to the territory of the member states for study purposes (OJ C 274, Vol. 39, of 19 September 1996).

35. Council Recommendation of 1–2 June 1993 concerning checks on and expulsion of third-country nationals residing or working without authorisation.

36. Council Resolution of 1–2 June 1993 on harmonisation of national policies on family reunification.

37. Abbreviation for 'Centre d'Information de Réflexion et d'Echange en Matière d'Asile', established by the Ad Hoc Group Immigration.

38. Apart from CIREA, a second centre for immigration, discussion and exchange on the crossing of frontiers and immigration (CIREFI) has been established, which does not deal with asylum seekers. An additional information system concerning asylum seekers is the European automated fingerprint recognition system (EURODAC), which shall complement a computerised list of undesired aliens.

39. Ad Hoc Group Immigration, Draft Resolution on Manifestly Unfounded Applications for Asylum, Progress Report on discussions in the Asylum Sub-Group. Note by the Presidency, 1 November 1992, SN 3926/92 WGI 1195 AS 128 (quoted in Joly 1996: 55).

40. The use of the 'safe third country' notion is not completely new. Since the 1980s, it has been applied by several European states under different labels such as 'first country of asylum' or 'first host country'. However, these notions did in general either presuppose the fact that the asylum seeker had been granted asylum in that country before or that he or she had spent a considerable time in its territory. With the London Resolution, the use of this rule has been harmonised and systematised in restrictive terms.

41. This is an implicit reference to Art. 3 of the European Convention on Human Rights and Fundamental Freedoms (see Chapter 1).

42. Report from the Ministers Responsible for Immigration to the European Council meeting in Maastricht on immigration and asylum policy.

43. Joint position of 4 March 1996 on the harmonised application of the definition of the term 'refugee' in Art. 1 of the Geneva Convention of 28 July 1951 relating to the status of refugees.

44. Refugees 'sur place' are persons who did not fear persecution at the moment of leaving their country of origin but who, given to changes of the situation in their country of origin since their departure, cannot return because of a well-founded fear of persecution.

45. See the critiques by ECRE (1995), the Standing Committee of Experts (1994), and UNHCR (1995c).

46. According to the UNHCR, in 1994 Germany hosted around 400,000 refugees, while for example Italy hosted 40,000 and Greece and Portugal 100 each (quoted in Thorburn 1995: 462).

47. Adopted by the European Council in Copenhagen on 1 June 1993.

48. In particular, the Council of Europe dealt a great deal with the development of a solidaristic approach to refugees from the former Yugoslavia.

49. Examples of these 'safe havens' are the cities of Srebrenica, Bihac, Gorazde, Mostar, Sarajevo and Tuzla in Bosnia-Herzegovina, where both UNHCR and other humanitarian agencies have constantly complained of the unsafe conditions (Thorburn 1995: 470–71).

50. Resolution on the Right of Asylum of 12 March 1987 (OJ C 099 of 13 April 1987), and the Resolution on the Asylum Policy of Certain Member States of 18 June 1987 (OJ C190 of 20 July 1987).

51. Resolution on the Harmonisation within the European Community of Asylum Law and Policies of 18 November 1992 (OJ C 337 of 21 December 1992). At the same time, a second Resolution on European Immigration Policy was issued (OJ C337 of 21 December 1992).

52. Document A3-0402/93 of 3 December 1993.

53. COM(1988) 640.

54. SEC(91) 1857 final.

55. See attached Declaration No. 31 on Justice and Home Affairs.

56. Commission Report on the possibility of applying Art. K.9 of 4 November 1993, SEC(93) 1687 final.

57. COM(94) 23 final.

58. COM(94) para. 85.

3 The Extension of the EU Refugee Regime

Since the opening up of the Eastern bloc, Western European countries have demonstrated a vivid interest in limiting immigration from the East and in tightening up the newly liberalised Eastern borders. This was motivated by the perceived threat posed by large-scale immigration of newly liberated citizens from these countries, and the realisation that with the liberalisation of their borders, the latter were likely to become a major transit zone for immigrants and refugees from the East and South. These fears reflected a general shift towards the restriction of immigration to Western Europe through the strengthening of external borders, the enhancement of control capacities, and the establishment of a redistributive mechanism for handling asylum claims. From this perspective, the opening up of the Eastern bloc represented not only the additional threat of potential immigrants, but constituted a challenge to intergovernmental co-operation amongst EU member states. The strategy adopted by Western Europe to deal with these perceived threats has been to unilaterally incorporate the countries of Central and Eastern Europe (CEECs)[1] into their emerging refugee regime through the extension of the redistributive system for handling asylum claims and the export of high standards of border-control technology.

Considering that the vast majority of immigrants and refugees arriving by land cross the CEECs in order to reach Western Europe, increasingly restrictive immigration and asylum policies in the West and the application of the 'safe third country' rule have effectively increased the number of migrants who stay in the former transit countries. This rapid transition of the CEECs from countries of transit and emigration to countries of immigration is reinforced by the many bilateral and multilateral activities designed to export EU asylum and immigration policies to the CEECs.

In practice, the extension of the EU refugee regime occurs at various levels and covers a wide variety of activities. Broadly speaking, one can distinguish between the bilateral activities of single countries, co-ordinated initiatives at the EU intergovernmental level, multilateral processes, and measures taken within the framework of EU enlargement. These processes focus on two main issues: the fight against illegal immigration and the strengthening of Eastern borders through the development of common standards of control and technology; and asylum matters *per se* through the establishment of basic legislative, administrative and social infrastructure for the protection of refugees.

These developments have multiple, and partly contradictory, effects. On the one hand, the introduction of specific regulations regarding asylum seekers indicates the adherence of the newly democratised countries to liberal values and their accession to the co-operative framework of the international refugee regime. On the other hand, this liberal turn threatens to be undermined by the very dynamics that helped generate it in so far as the CEECs' transformation into countries of immigration is to a great extent dictated by the concerns of Western European countries with illegal immigration and their exposure to Incoming refugee flows. As a consequence, accession of the CEECs to the international system of co-operation for the protection of refugees is shaped by two conflicting paradigms: the liberal values of the international refugee regime on the one hand, and the restrictionist limitation of immigration flows of the contemporary EU refugee regime on the other.

The central thesis of this chapter is that within the political context of a future enlargement of the Union, the restrictionist paradigm tends to take precedence over the liberal one. Three dynamics are identified as being particularly relevant in these processes: the interest of Western European states in sealing the eastern borders, promoted in various bilateral and multilateral processes; the CEECs' concern with their transformation into a 'buffer zone' warding off unwanted aliens on their way to Western Europe; and the dynamics of EU enlargement, which have made the CEECs' adaptation to the restrictive 'acquis'[2] in the fields of asylum and immigration a central issue in pre-accession strategies. In this context, the problem of preventing own citizens and third-country nationals from entering Western Europe is likely to become a significant obstacle to an early eastward enlargement and will inhibit the introduction of free movement between East and West for an indeterminate period of time.

THE EXPORT OF ASYLUM AND IMMIGRATION POLICIES: INTERGOVERNMENTAL PROCESSES

In analysing the various initiatives of Western European states designed to extend the European refugee regime to Central and Eastern Europe, a distinction has been made between purely unilateral and bilateral activities, such as the adoption of the 'safe third country' rule and the conclusion of readmission agreements, co-ordinated initiatives of the EU member states taken under the third pillar of the Maastricht Treaty and the various overarching multilateral activities which include not only EU member states, but also other European and non-European countries together with international organisations and NGOs.

Unilateral and Bilateral Activities

The extension of the EU refugee regime is not so much a result of the CEECs' shift towards democratic values or a necessary consequence of an expanding European integration as it is an attempt by Western European countries to expand their fight against illegal immigration and to reduce the number of asylum seekers on their territory. Accordingly, the first activities implying an involvement of CEECs were initiated by individual Western European countries at a unilateral and bilateral level. These activities concentrate firstly on measures regarded as necessary for the implementation of the 'safe third country' rule, and secondly on the transfer of funds and technology for the fight against illegal immigration and the establishment of basic legal and administrative infrastructure for the treatment of refugees.

THE ADOPTION OF THE 'SAFE THIRD COUNTRY' RULE

With the adoption of the 'safe third country' rule in national legislation, the EU member states have unilaterally incorporated third countries outside their legal and political domain, such as the CEECs, into their system of redistribution for handling asylum claims (Lavenex 1998a). In principle, this rule denies access to substantive status determination procedure on the grounds that the asylum seeker has already found, or could reasonably have been expected to find, protection in another country. The application of this rule, however, varies considerably. Even after the adoption of the 1992 London Resolution, these was no consensus on how to define the concept of 'safe' when applying the rule, nor do EU member states apply the same criteria for denying access to asylum procedures on 'safe third country' grounds.[3] In general, this rule may be applied either more or less restrictively, depending on the level of evidence required to determine the country as 'safe', the length of stay in the third country required to apply the rule, the opportunity for the independent legal review of the denial of entry or asylum, and the concrete procedural safeguards applied when rejecting an asylum seeker on the grounds of the 'safe third country' rule.

With regard to the definition of a 'safe' country, member states' practice extends from the requirement of the existence of fair and equitable asylum procedures in accordance with the Geneva Convention and the European Convention on Human Rights, and the requirement of the consent of the readmitting state to examine the asylum seeker's claim to less far-reaching requirements, such as the fact that the country has signed the Geneva Convention. In some countries, the fact that an asylum seeker has crossed such a 'safe' country before does not automatically preclude that person from having his or her case examined. Instead, these claims are processed in accelerated procedures. According to the London Resolution, the mere transit through a third state may be sufficient to assume that the asylum seeker has had the opportunity to claim asylum there, whereas some countries require that the person has spent a certain period there which can amount to a minimum of three months.

Another major point of difference between member states' practices relates to the opportunity to lodge an appeal against a rejection on the basis of this rule. Here again, the variety of regulations range from a complete absence of review mechanisms to the existence of appeal procedures without suspensive effect–meaning that the asylum claimant has to leave the country during the review–and finally review procedures with suspensive effect. Finally, the organisation of the return process itself deserves attention because it can seriously affect the opportunity of the rejected asylum seeker to lodge an asylum claim in the third country. While in most countries, neither the rejected applicant nor the receiving country are informed about the reason for his or her rejection and about the fact that their asylum application has not been examined on substantive grounds, a limited number of member states provide comprehensive safeguards to ensure that the asylum seeker will have their claim examined in the third country. This includes the information given to the asylum seeker about the reason for refusal, the address and telephone number of the UNHCR office in the third country concerned and of a refugee-assisting NGO, as well as a written statement in the language of that country to be submitted to the receiving authorities, stating that the returned person has been rejected on 'safe third country' grounds alone, that his or her asylum claim has not been examined on its merits and that he or she wishes to apply for asylum in the third country.

As these examples show, one cannot speak of a harmonised 'safe third country' concept in Western European asylum laws and practices. In addition to these conceptual differences, the *de facto* implementation of this rule has proved difficult for all the states mentioned, for two reasons. The first is a practical reason caused by the difficulty of identifying the travel route pursued by the asylum seeker and the fact that, fearing rejection, many asylum seekers try to conceal where they have come from. Another more conceptual reason, however, is that the 'safe third country' rule has no foundation in international law (Fortin 1993).[4] International customary law imposes the obligation on states to take back their *own* citizens, but not third-country nationals. Furthermore, the member states introduced this rule in their national legislation unilaterally without consulting the third states concerned on their willingness and ability to participate in this system of redistribution. This lack of a legal basis has been resolved by the conclusion of bilateral readmission agreements between the member states and third countries as a legal means to ensure the participation of the receiving state.

READMISSION AGREEMENTS

The conclusion of readmission agreements with third countries is an additional instrument in the implementation of the extending EU refugee regime with two functions. Firstly, it is a necessary legal instrument for the implementation of the 'safe third country' rule and thus the extension of the redistributive system for the examination of asylum claims first established with the Schengen and Dublin Conventions to non-EU countries. The second function relates to the implementation of the London Conclusions on safe countries of origin and is designed to facilitate the expulsion of rejected asylum seekers and illegal immigrants to their home country.

The recent readmission agreements signed between Western and Central-Eastern European countries must be distinguished from earlier readmission agreements between Western European states of the 1950s and 1960s. The 'old' type of readmission agreements already contained the duty to readmit own-state nationals as well as foreigners who had entered the territory of the requesting party illegally. Although the obligation to readmit own-state nationals is already a norm in international law, these agreements intended to expedite the procedures of return, especially with regard to the formal proofs required to establish the nationality of the person concerned (Schieffer 1997: 101).[5] In general, the readmission was made conditional on the requirement that the person had previously spent a certain period in the requested country. With regard to refugees, these agreements could only apply to asylum seekers whose applications had been rejected in last instance.

By the 1990s, this type of agreement was perceived as largely unsatisfactory. Their efficacy was mainly hindered by the difficulty of providing evidence for the illegal entry of the aliens. The necessary documents were often missing, and legal differences in the interpretation of the conditions of illegal entry between the requesting and the requested country often made readmission unfeasible. As a result, readmissions were rarely executed, or the persons concerned were sent back and forth from one country to another (Hailbronner 1996: 54–55).

The new generation of readmission agreement is designed to facilitate the expulsion of non-EU nationals, including–although this is rarely made explicit–asylum seekers on the grounds of the 'safe country of origin' and the 'safe third country' rules. The conclusion of such agreements between EU member states and so-called 'safe third countries' has its conceptual roots in the redistributive mechanism of the Dublin and Schengen Conventions signed by the EU member states. This mechanism is based on the idea that the first country which has enabled the (legal or illegal) entry of an asylum seeker shall take that person back.

Many of these bilateral agreements have been modelled on the readmission agreement concluded by the Schengen states with Poland in 1991. They depart from earlier agreements in four major respects. Firstly, these new agreements may also be applied to asylum seekers who have been denied entry at the border on the basis of the 'safe third country' rule and whose claim has not yet been considered on substantive grounds. Under this rule, they can be subsumed within the general category of third-country nationals, which clearly does not take their specific situation into consideration, that is, the obligation to allow them access to asylum procedures. A second general difference is that whereas before, readmission agreements were mainly concluded amongst countries of immigration, the new generation is focused on transit countries and directly on the countries of emigration. The implicit consequence is their one-way application as an instrument of the main countries of immigration to return undesired aliens. At a more procedural level, a third important difference concerns formal requirements for the application of the readmission procedure, in so far as the new agreements tend to minimise the readmission requirements, such as, for example, the abolition of the specified period of stay of the individual in the requested state or the reduction of the level of proof required to establish the obligation of the re-admitting party. The agreements normally contain detailed provisions on the means for the establishment of such evidence such as an official certification issued at the border, observations made in travel documents, train or airline tickets, and declarations on the applicant's entry made by persons such as border officials. Other reliable indications are verifiable statements made by the applicant, bills, receipts, or other written documents which indicate that the person has been present in the requested country. In order to comply with these formalities necessary for the efficient application of the readmission agreements, Western European states try to avoid the imposition of time limits in readmission requirements. A last important feature of the new generation of readmission agreements is the basis for the obligation of readmission, which is no longer established by the illegal crossing of the common border between the contracting states but also requires readmission when a person entered the requesting country lawfully, provided that the person is now remaining unlawfully. This corresponds to Article 2 of the readmission agreement between Poland and the Schengen countries, which stipulates that, 'At the request of a contracting party, the contracting party whose external border was the point of entry of the person who does not fulfil or who no longer fulfils the entry or visit conditions applicable within the territory of the requesting contracting party, shall readmit that person into its territory without formalities.'

Most EU member states have now concluded readmission agreements with the associated CEECs[6] which apply either to the readmission of own-state nationals or to the readmission of own-state nationals including third-country nationals.

The first category of agreements are designed to implement the 'safe country of origin' rule in the case of asylum seekers or at the facilitated return of illegal immigrants to their home country in general. Fearing large flows of immigrants from Central and Eastern Europe, some member states have explicitly designated several countries of Central and Eastern Europe as safe in the sense of the London Conclusions of 1992 (see Chapter 2).[7]

By way of example,[8] Germany, given its geographical position and its situation as a major destination country for asylum seekers and voluntary migrants from Central-Eastern Europe, has taken the lead in these matters and concluded agreements with Romania (24 September 1994), Bulgaria (9 September 1994), Croatia (25 April 1994), the Federal Republic of Yugoslavia (10 October 1996), and non-European countries, *inter alia* Vietnam, Pakistan and Algeria.[9] Since many persons seeking asylum in Germany originate from these countries, the goal of the agreements is a swift and bureaucratically streamlined return following the rejection of a claim in an accelerated procedure. This appears to work well–according to the German Ministry of the Interior, in 1992 Germany still hosted some 100,000 asylum seekers from Romania, but by 1993 the numbers had fallen to 73,000 and subsequently to 3,500 in 1995. Between 1993 and 1995, approximately 85,000 persons were returned to Romania by air on the basis of this agreement (Schieffer 1997: 102).

The second group of readmission treaties also regards third-state nationals. Although often not mentioned explicitly, it is generally assumed that these readmission agreements provide the legal basis for the rejection of asylum seekers whose application has not yet been examined on the grounds of the 'safe third country' rule. In Germany, such agreements have been signed with Poland (7 May 1993) and the Czech Republic (9 November 1994).[10] Since these agreements are logically to the debit of the CEECs, which have become important transit countries for asylum seekers and voluntary migrants heading West, they are usually accompanied by the lifting of visa requirements between the contracting parties and the provision of material aid on part of Western states. The implementation of these agreements not only presupposes the existence of equitable asylum systems in the third country but is accompanied by a strengthening of territorial borders and the adoption of high standards of border control technology. As a consequence, Germany has concluded additional co-operation agreements for the fight against illegal immigration. In this framework, 120 million DM has been transferred to Poland, which has borders with Germany, Belarus and the Ukraine, and 60 million DM to the Czech Republic. These funds are intended to 'diminish the financial burden resulting from the amendment of the German asylum law and the readmission agreement(s)' and to enhance border protection and establish infrastructure for coping with asylum seekers and refugees (Schieffer 1997: 194).

SEALING THE EASTERN BORDERS

The implementation of the 'safe third country' rule and the conclusion of readmission agreements were accompanied by a wide range of related bilateral co-operation processes between single EU member states and CEECs which focus on the enforcement of Eastern borders and the setting up of an efficient infrastructure for the fight against illegal immigration.

These activities are part of a spreading field of international co-operation for the safeguarding of 'internal security'. Fearing an increase in illegal activities commonly subsumed under the term of 'organised crime', Western states have engaged in a new form of development aid which is geared to the transformation and development of the state monopoly of force in the CEECs, in particular the police and secret services. The main targets of this co-operation are not only the 'classical' trans-national concerns such as illegal trafficking in drugs and weapons, but first and foremost also the fight against the illegal entry and 'smuggling' of voluntary and forced migrants, which is increasingly being subsumed under the heading of organised crime.[11] This new field of co-operation tends to follow the interests of the Western states and leads to an approximation of threat perceptions, concepts and methods in the CEECs to Western patterns.

Given its focus on the fight against illegal immigration, this co-operation includes the strengthening of national borders through technological innovation, the training of police and border guards, the introduction of information and communication systems, and changes to criminal law, for example, the effective punishment of trafficking in human beings or the falsification or forging of documents.

Despite its ongoing expansion, co-operation among Western and Central-Eastern European police forces has remained uncoordinated and occurs mainly on a bilateral basis. Again, the most active country in these matters is Germany. According to the German Ministry of the Interior, in 1995 more than 2 million DM were invested in general border equipment in the CEECs such as motor vehicles; photographic, video, and radio equipment; fax machines; night vision devices; mobile telephones; and forensic equipment. For the same year, expenditure on training in internal security matters amounted to around 600,000 DM, and an additional sum of around 70,000 DM was invested in general advice measures.

The country with which Germany has developed this form of co-operation to the greatest extent is Poland, with which it shares the longest part of its Eastern border. While backed by a series of intergovernmental agreements and protocols among the two countries, this co-operation has evolved predominantly at an informal level in direct contacts between German and Polish police officials (Busch 1996b; Dietrich 1998).[12] This co-operation is mainly financed by the bilateral readmission agreement between Germany and Poland concluded in 1993. From the total 120 million DM, almost half, has been allocated to the border authorities for the enforcement of the frontier, while another 38 per cent has been earmarked for the police.[13]

Although not overtly linked to the question of asylum seekers and refugees, these measures are of crucial importance for all persons seeking to cross the border, since their main objective is to limit migration both from and through these countries into Western Europe. Accordingly, one of the dominant concerns in these processes is the fight against individuals and organisations which assist immigrants in crossing borders illegally. The emergence of this relatively new phenomenon of 'human smuggling' is partly due to the adoption of increasingly restrictive entry requirements in the West. Because this is perceived as one of the major threats for the stability of Western societies, it is now officially referred to as one of the central features of 'organised crime' in Europe.[14] In spring 1998, the co-operation between Poland and Germany acquired a new dimension when the German Minister of the Interior deployed–without any contractual basis[15]–a group of border police officials on the Polish side of the border to support their Polish counterparts in the fight against illegal immigration (*Frankfurter Rundschau,* 18 August 1998). In addition, several related private initiatives were granted support from the national TRANSFORM programme, which was originally designed to support the general transition to democracy and the free market economy.

Apart from Germany, other member states such as Austria, France, Italy and the Scandinavian countries have also engaged in this field of co-operation. In particular, they organise

exchange programmes for Central and Eastern European po-
licemen and senior officials dealing with immigration-related
matters such as document forgery, airport security, migration
flows and the Schengen provisions. Although there is little clarity over the concrete scope and contents of these processes
given their often informal nature, it appears that they follow
clearly geographical criteria. Thus, while Germany has focused
on Poland and, to a lesser degree, the Czech Republic, Austria
and Italy concentrate their efforts on Hungary and Slovenia,
while the Scandinavian countries co-operate almost exclusively
on the Baltic states. The need to co-ordinate these activities
has led to the establishment of multilateral consultations among
the Ministries of the Interior of all countries concerned, which
have materialised in what is known as the Budapest Group.
Furthermore, with the prospect of EU enlargement, most of
these activities have been put on the agenda of the Union in its
pre-accession strategies with Central-Eastern Europe.

In sum, this co-operation in police and border matters is of
the utmost importance since it concerns the core of state sovereignty, namely the state's monopoly over the means of violence and the control of its territorial borders. These processes,
dominated by Western efforts to incorporate their Central-
Eastern European neighbours in the prevention of perceived
threats, these processes amount to a serious interference in
these states' internal and home affairs and to their unilateral
adaptation to Western perceptions of threat and Western operative methods. Nowhere is this predominance of EU member
states' interests clearer than in the fields of immigration and
asylum, which would not constitute a major concern in the
CEECs without pressure from the EU.

THE ESTABLISHMENT OF ASYLUM SYSTEMS

The existence of equitable asylum systems in the third countries is imperative for the implementation of the 'safe third
country' rule and the introduction of readmission agreements,

coupled with co-operation in border enforcement measures. Compared with the co-operation in police and border enforcement matters, aid for asylum-related matters occupies a much smaller place in the bilateral activities between EU member states and CEECs. This is reflected in the limited scope of these activities, and in the fact that they started only relatively late and notably only after EU member states had designated some CEECs as 'safe' in the sense of the 'safe third country' rule. Co-operation in this field originated in the realisation that the effective implementation of this rule, and hence the extension of the system of redistribution for handling asylum claims to the CEECs, required the existence of a basic legal, administrative and social infrastructure. This need resulted from the fact that the CEECs not only lacked the common Western European tradition in these matters, but also the norms, practices and institutions for the protection of refugees which would be required for their definition as 'safe'.

From an international relations perspective, this evolving co-operation between EU member states and CEECs in asylum matters follows several, and in some instances contradictory objectives. On the one hand, the involvement of the CEECs in the system of refugee protection supports their accession to the international refugee regime as a broader co-operative framework rooted in the United Nations system. On the other hand, however, the commitment of these countries to the principles, norms and rules of the international refugee regime are undermined by the very dynamics which support their accession to the regime. Given the focus on the fight against illegal immigration and bogus asylum seekers, this dynamic shifts the emphasis away from the humanitarian foundations of refugee law towards control and restrictive measures. By favouring restrictions to freedoms, the bilateral activities which induced the adoption of asylum laws and regulations by the CEECs thus tend to run counter to the liberal spirit of international refugee protection.

The underlying logic of these processes can be summarised in the following manner: since the application of both the 'safe third country' and the 'safe country of origin' concepts presuppose a certain level of legal compliance with international human rights norms, Western states have helped the CEECs to fulfil the requirements of the Geneva Refugee Convention and the European Convention on Human Rights and Fundamental Freedoms as a necessary condition for the implementation of these two cornerstones of the expanding EU refugee regime. Yet this normative necessity also has a strategic dimension: helping the associated countries join the system of international protection for refugees is an attractive way to redistribute responsibility. Given the geographical position of most CEECs as transit countries for migrants and asylum seekers from the South and the East on their way to Western Europe, both the establishment of equitable asylum systems and the application of the 'safe third country' rule are important instruments for the reduction of the numbers of asylum seekers lodging applications in the West.

According to information provided by the European Commission, by March 1997, eight member states were conducting bilateral support programmes related to asylum matters with the associated CEECs. The review of these co-operation programmes illustrates their close connection with the national interests of the respective member states: with the exceptions of France and the Netherlands, which are surrounded by EU member states, these exchanges follow the criteria of geographical proximity. Here, their complementarity with the aim of implementing the 'safe third country' rule and readmission agreements becomes apparent. For instance, the Nordic countries concentrate their efforts on the Baltic states. The Danish Immigration Service runs seminars, training programmes and consultancy on refugee issues for the Baltic states, and the Danish government provides technical assistance and financial support to the Lithuanian government for the development of a migrant/refugee reception centre and practical training in refugee status determination to Lithuanian officials. Finland co-operates mainly with Estonia and has provided support to the Estonian Migration Board for the processing of residence applications and is planning to provide technical assistance on the development of immigration and refugee policy and establish a centralised passport register. In addition, it also provides Lithuanian refugee centres with material support. Sweden provides technical support and seminars on the development of migration and refugee policies for the Baltic states and has provided material support for the refugee centres in Latvia and Lithuania. Finally, all three countries co-operate with the Netherlands in supporting the International Organisation for Migration's programme for the Baltic states (see section on the IOM below). On a bilateral basis, the Dutch Ministry of Justice has signed mutual co-operation Memoranda of Understanding with the national migration services of Poland and the Czech Republic.

Once again, Germany has played a leading role, but compared with the efforts made in the field of police and border co-operation, activities related to asylum seekers occupy a subordinate place on the policy agenda. This is best reflected in the fact that, from the 120 million DM offered to Poland in the context of the bilateral readmission agreements, only a very small part, namely 13 per cent, was earmarked for asylum infrastructure (*Bundestagsdrucksache* 13/6030, 30 Oct. 1996). Germany has set up co-operation programmes for seminars and training between its Federal Office for the Recognition of Foreign Refugees, the central administrative agency dealing with asylum claims, and several CEECs, including Bulgaria, Lithuania, the Czech Republic and Slovakia and Poland (EC Commission 1997a: Annex III, 1). The general focus of these programmes is to draft or reform asylum laws and establish an efficient administrative structure to process asylum claims, compatible with the EU 'acquis' in this field. An important part of this co-operation consists of the exchange of information on the countries of origin. This is supported by concrete co-operation in the processing of asylum claims, both in the administrative and judicial procedure. A second major area of exchange consists of the training of officials dealing with asylum seekers and refugees, both in the countries themselves or through internships in German offices. As in the case of border enforcement measures, this co-operation is supported by the TRANSFORM programme (Adling and Jahn 1997).

The review of these bilateral co-operation processes reveals some of the major dynamics leading to an extension of the EU refugee regime to Central and Eastern Europe. First, EU member states have unilaterally incorporated the CEECs into their redistributive system for handling asylum claims via the 'safe country' rules without seeking their consent. It was only after these rules had been adopted in domestic asylum laws that member states realised that their effective implementation required the consent and co-operation of the readmitting country. The legal and political basis for the bureaucratically streamlined return of own-country and third-country nationals to CEECs was established with the conclusion of readmission agreements.

In addition to these two concrete instruments, the extension of the EU refugee regime is embedded in a vast series of activities in the field of police co-operation, border enforcement and asylum and immigration policy. The focus of these activities is predominantly on the fight against illegal immigration, including the tightening of border controls, the fight against human smuggling and the strengthening of the related administrative and judicial infrastructure. In comparison, the promotion of refugee law and the establishment of an administrative, institutional and social infrastructure for the protection of refugees and other migrants in accordance with humanitarian standards received much less support.

These examples indicate that the consent of the CEECs to participation in a pan-European refugee regime based on EU member states' interests was not altogether voluntary. According to a German official from the Ministry of the Interior, 'some states [...] refuse to co-operate for political reasons or–openly or covertly–make readmission contingent on visa facilitations or financial considerations,' so that 'it seems reasonable to attempt to convince the relevant states of the significance of readmission agreements in order to ensure the rapid and simplified termination of residence by means of such agreements.' (Schieffer 1997: 99). However, this consent is not only linked to financial and technological transfers but must, more importantly, be interpreted in the light of the linkage of immigration and asylum matters with the prospect of membership of the European Union.

The EU Intergovernmental Level

Before raising the question of EU enlargement, we should have a look at the level of multilateral intergovernmental co-operation and the extension of the European refugee regime in the context of the Schengen and Dublin Conventions and the ongoing harmonisation under the Treaty on the European Union. Again, the bilateral activities examined above do not occur in an isolated environment, but are firmly linked to the work of the intergovernmental forums of the EU member states dealing with asylum and immigration. As already mentioned, the efforts made under the third pillar of the Maastricht Treaty to harmonise external aspects of asylum and immigration policies can be traced back to the Schengen and the Dublin Conventions of 1990. Both these agreements contain provisions which indicate the willingness to extend the system of redistribution for handling asylum claims to other, non-EU countries—and this despite the repeated assertion that their impact on the field of asylum would be limited. Taking a longitudinal perspective, one can draw a line from these first agreements to the adoption of the 'safe third country' rule and subsequently the harmonisation of policies towards safe countries. Parallel to the activities pursued at the national level, the intergovernmental groups have started to develop a common approach for the countries of Central and Eastern Europe to encourage the effective implementation of the 'safe third country' rule. To this end, they have taken steps to harmonise the return of rejected aliens and are developing common guidelines for the conclusion of readmission agreements.

EARLY SIGNS OF EXTENSION: SCHENGEN, DUBLIN AND THIRD COUNTRIES

The Schengen and the Dublin Conventions, which set up a system of redistribution based on the 'safe third country' rule, were originally limited to EU member states. However, the interest of some of these countries to include third parties was evident early on. As a member of the Nordic Union, Denmark had an immediate interest in the adhesion of the non-EU Nordic states to the Dublin Convention. However, it was found that the linkage of this treaty with the Community's single market restricted full membership to EU members. Instead, a parallel convention was drafted for the participation of Norway, Sweden and also Switzerland that is virtually the same as the original. With the delay in the entering into force of the Dublin Convention, these parallel agreements were suspended and negotiations have only recently been restarted, although it appears that they will be limited to the former EFTA countries.

In the Schengen group, the incorporation of non-EU countries has already materialised more concretely. An adhesion of the Nordic EFTA states, Norway and Iceland, and hence the incorporation of the Nordic Union into the group, was agreed in 1998. With regard to the CEECs, it seems that the Schengen states also oppose the extension of the treaty. Instead, these states have anticipated the incorporation of Central European countries into the refugee regime with the signing of a readmission agreement with Poland on 29 March 1991 that aims at the return of illegal immigrants who enter 'Schengenland' via Poland. This agreement has to be considered as a sort of package deal for lifting visa requirements for tourist purposes; that is to say, Poland signed this agreement in exchange for visa-free travel for Polish citizens to Schengen countries. It serves as a model for newer bilateral agreements. In particular, the agreements concluded by Germany have followed its example. Since it applies not only to citizens of the contracting parties, but also to third-country nationals, including asylum seekers who passed through Polish territory, it corresponds roughly with the redistributive mechanism of the Schengen and the Dublin Conventions (Czaplinski 1994: 641). Basically, it is designed to encourage the rapid and informal rejection of unauthorised persons arriving via Poland from the Schengen states. The deadlines and procedures for the request to readmit an individual and for his or her admission are swift and unbureaucratic. By fixing a legal commitment for readmission, this agreement anticipates the application of the 'safe third country' rule and can hence be interpreted as a forerunner of EU-wide co-operation.

This interpretation is supported by a second element of the Schengen Convention, also included in the Dublin Convention–the provision that member states retain the right to return asylum seekers to third countries in line with their national legislation. Together with the Schengen-Poland agreement, this provision has paved the way for a harmonised approach to safe third countries as adopted in the London Resolution and the subsequent conclusion of bilateral readmission agreements with the third countries concerned.

ACTIVITIES UNDER THE THIRD PILLAR: THE HARMONISATION OF READMISSION AGREEMENTS

The spread of bilateral readmission agreements has induced the member states to take measures to harmonise these new instruments in the fight against illegal immigration and the redistribution of asylum seekers. These measures, taken under the third pillar of the Maastricht Treaty, have been largely inspired by the German experience with its Eastern neighbours and the principles developed in the multilateral Schengen readmission agreement with Poland. They are part of the broader attempt to harmonise the questions of repatriation and extradition.

The issue of readmission came onto the agenda of the Ministers of Justice and Home Affairs at their first meeting under the third pillar in late 1993. An Action Programme was adopted which provided for the establishment of general principles for the conclusion of bilateral and multilateral readmission agreements. Furthermore, the opportunity to link the question of re-admission with the Co-operation, Association and Europe Agreements concluded between the Community and its member states with third countries was proposed. According to an official from the German Ministry of the Interior, 'the idea [...] is to have additional means to exert influence with a view to the readmission of nationals of the other party residing illegally in the territory of a Member State.' (Schieffer 1997: 107). This Action Programme was approved by the European Council in December 1993 and was drafted by the competent working groups of the Council without consultation with the European Parliament.

The first result of these endeavours is the Draft Council Recommendation concerning a Specimen Bilateral Readmission Agreement between a Member State of the European Union and a Third Country adopted at the behest of Germany at the Council of Justice and Home Affairs Ministers on 30 November–1 December 1994. Although the advantages of concluding comprehensive multilateral readmission agreements were recognised, the Ministers preferred to design a 'model' bilateral agreement which is usually concluded more rapidly and used in a more flexible manner in accordance with the specific interests of the contracting parties. The legal nature of this instrument is again very questionable. Not only did the Ministers fail–as with the London and other conclusions and resolutions–to use the formal instruments provided under the third pillar (Art. K.1, paragraph 2 a–c), but also the prefix 'draft' contributes to the obscurity of its status.

The suggested 'specimen' follows largely the example of the Schengen-Poland Agreement. It applies both to own-state nationals and third-country nationals and can be applied in the case of transit where direct return to the country of origin is not feasible. The Draft is supplemented by an agreement on principles for the drafting of protocols on the implementation of such agreements reached under the French Presidency in June 1995. The 'specimen readmission agreement' has been sharply criticised by the European Parliament.[16] Apart from formal disagreement concerning the secrecy and the obscure legal nature with which it has been negotiated, the report by the European Parliament contains important substantive points. With regard to the application of the 'safe third country' rule, the main weakness of this attempt at harmonisation is the fact that it fails to specify any specific safeguards which take the particular situation and needs of asylum seekers into consideration. This category of persons is not even mentioned in the draft specimen, although its Article 11 implicitly confirms its applicability to asylum seekers when it stipulates that the Geneva Convention of 1951, as well as the European Convention of Human Rights and Fundamental Freedoms and other international conventions on asylum including the Dublin Convention, shall not be affected by it. Respecting these conventions, however, would presuppose the introduction of certain substantive and procedural standards for the readmission of refugees, such as, for example, informing the asylum seeker of the reason for his or her rejection at the border, communicating to the relevant authorities of the readmitting party that the asylum seeker's claim has not been examined on substantive grounds, and finally affirming that the asylum request will be examined by the readmitting party.

The normative and legal criticisms of attempts to incorporate Central and Eastern European countries into the system of redistribution for handling refugees are backed up by an alternative proposal of a draft skeleton readmission agreement made by the Czech Republic in 1995.[17] This document starts by stipulating that a multilateral agreement, giving equal consideration to the interests of the Central European countries, should be aimed for. Its central theme is the detection of fundamental differences between the position of Western European states and those of Eastern or Central Europe. The following quotation hits the nail on the head. According to the Czech Republic, 'it is understandable that Western European countries favour the "broadest" possible obligations, as they are mostly destination countries. Compared to that, the Central and East European countries–and mainly the transit countries–are determined by their worries of overfilling their territories with illegal migrants returned from Western Europe'.[18] Hence, these countries see themselves as a 'buffer zone' for illegal immigrants seeking to reach Western Europe. In the interest of the 'good co-operation practice' among European countries, however, the document expresses the intention to help EU countries, if these are in return prepared to assist the CEECs, for example, through the provision of 'financial reimbursement for the consequences of illegal migration.' From the Czech point of view, 'this can be understood as burden-sharing in the context of illegal migration in Europe.' On top of these declarations, the document expresses a clear and fundamental critique of the previous unilateral application of the 'safe third country' rule when it states that its application affects 'countries which have not been consulted on this approach'.

The consequence of the CEECs' unilateral incorporation into the European refugee regime is clear: they will actively engage in the conclusion of readmission agreements with their Eastern and Southern neighbours–and alleviate their exposure to migration flows by establishing a 'chain of readmission agreements'.

Apart from this intergovernmental co-operation amongst EU countries, the issue of asylum policy in the CEECs has appeared on the agendas of several multilateral forums involving other European and non-European countries as well as international organisations and NGOs.

Overarching Multilateral Activities

The intergovernmental and bilateral activities presented above are surrounded by a broader framework of East-West co-operation in the fields of asylum and immigration. The multitude of conferences, discussions and projects dealing with these issues is the expression of the central importance they have gained not only for national governments, but also for a large number of international organisations and NGOs. Induced by the fall of Communism and the fear of a mass exodus from the East to the West, it was soon realised that these fears would not materialise—and co-operation split up in a variety of forums with different perspectives and goals. Generally speaking, one can distinguish two kinds of multilateral processes. The first are the activities of international organisations and NGOs, which, from a humanitarian perspective, seek to counteract the restrictive trend in expanding EU refugee and immigration policies and support the establishment of fair and equitable asylum procedures in the CEECs. In contrast to these processes, the extension of restrictive policies has transgressed the Union's borders and is also being promoted through a series of intergovernmental conferences regrouping representatives of the interior ministries of a large number of Western, Central and Eastern European countries which concentrate on the fight against illegal immigration.

Without claiming to be comprehensive, the sections that follow give an overview of the main multilateral activities contributing, on one side or the other, to the extension of the EU refugee regime.

THE UNITED NATIONS HIGH COMMISSIONER FOR REFUGEES (UNHCR)

The most active international organisation supporting the CEECs' accession to the system of international co-operation for the protection of refugees is the UNHCR, which is the organisation responsible for safeguarding the international refugee regime (see Chapter 1). After the fall of the Communist regimes, the UNHCR opened regional liaison offices in all CEECs in order to ensure that the enactment of refugee laws was consistent with international standards. Accordingly, it promotes the ratification of pertinent international treaties and, where possible, assists governments in drafting refugee legislation. This legislative advice is supplemented by a wide range of training activities for persons dealing with refugees such as border officials, members of the status determination authorities, NGOs and lawyers. The UNHCR also provides financial support for lawyers who assist and represent asylum seekers. Due to its presence in the countries and its close co-operation with the national governments, the UNHCR has been able to detect gaps in national asylum procedures and to improve the standards of refugee protection considerably. In addition, it co-operates closely with local and international NGOs with regard to the social conditions for asylum seekers and refugees during and after the status determination procedure. Given the often problematic economic and social conditions in these countries, these initiatives are of central importance and range from the provision of reception facilities or housing to the supply of medical services and vocational training for recognised refugees. Finally, starting from the lack of tradition in human rights and refugee matters prevailing in these newly democratised countries, a last important field of activity is the promotion of human rights education programmes and general public information emphasising tolerance, the acceptance of minorities and the integration of refugees (UNHCR 1996a; 1996b).

Another UNHCR activity which also, albeit more indirectly, affects the CEECs is the so-called 'CIS Conference' to address the problems of refugees, displaced persons, other forms of involuntary displacement and returnees in the countries of the Commonwealth of Independent States and relevant neighbouring states, including some CEECs. This conference, which is monitored in co-operation with the IOM and the OSCE (Organisation on Security and Co-operation in Europe) attempts to identify the problems of mass population movements in the region and to formulate solutions and practical programmes on a national, regional and international level.

In sum, the UNHCR is the most important actor promoting the general principles, norms, rules and procedures of the international refugee regime in the CEECs. Considering its early commitment in these countries, its activities have been an important compensation for the predominantly restrictive approach

of Western European countries and an indispensable complement in upholding the international refugee regime.

THE INTERNATIONAL ORGANISATION FOR MIGRATION (IOM)

Although focusing more broadly on the general phenomenon of
migration, the IOM has become a major actor assisting CEECs
in their transition towards countries of immigration. As a follow-
up to the conference organised by the Council of Europe on the
movement of persons from the CEECs in 1991, the IOM was
responsible for investigating the 'real' migratory potential in four
countries (Albania, Bulgaria, Russia and Ukraine). A survey
conducted in 1992/93 concluded that very few people actually
wanted to leave to become migrants.[19] In the aftermath of this
study, the IOM developed information dissemination programmes on the opportunities and difficulties of immigrating in
several CEECs. Since then, the activities of this organisation
have focused on the technical assistance of CEECs as well as
the former Soviet Union countries (CIS) in designing, developing and implementing comprehensive migration management
programmes and the establishment of an information Clearing
House on migration and displacement in Central Europe and
the CIS. In addition, the IOM has set up return programmes for
rejected asylum seekers in several CEECs, including Hungary
and Romania. Finally, another major field of activity is the joint
CIS Regional Conference organised in co-operation with the
UNHCR and the OSCE.

THE ORGANISATION ON SECURITY AND CO-OPERATION IN EUROPE (OSCE)

A relatively new development is the introduction of refugee and
immigration issues in the work of the OSCE.[20] This organisation
comprises fifty-five countries from Europe and North America.
Its mandate, laid down in the final Act of the 1975 Helsinki

Conference, includes three main areas of co-operation: security and military matters; economy, science, technology and environment; and human rights and humanitarian issues.

Although refugees were originally not an issue of co-operation in this forum, they have gained increasing importance in the 1990s, and the main body dealing with these issues, the Office for Democratic Institutions and Human Rights (ODIHR), is particularly active in holding seminars in the context of the CIS Conference.

The increasing activity of the OSCE in these matters started with the new focus on human rights objectives laid down in the Paris Charter of 1990. Two years later, a section dealing with refugees and displaced persons was included in the Helsinki document of 1992, which stresses the link between human rights violations and refugee movements as well as the importance of international co-operation for the prevention of root causes and the protection of refugees. In 1993, a Human Dimension Seminar on Migration, Including Refugees and Displaced Persons was held in Warsaw, which dealt with the prevention of involuntary migration, protection, and institution-building with a focus on temporary protection for refugees from the former Yugoslavia.

THE COUNCIL OF EUROPE

Both its humanitarian mandate and its early eastward enlargement have contributed to the Council of Europe's involvement in immigration and asylum matters in the CEECs, and the annual conferences of the European Ministers Responsible for Immigration are indicative of this development. At the meeting held in Warsaw in June 1996, the participating countries recognised that the CEECs had become destination countries themselves and that this was partly a result of the reinforcement of controls in other countries. As a consequence, the ministers made a commitment to pay more attention to the interests of the CEECs (Council of Europe 1996: 6).

Apart from these regular meetings, the Council of Europe provided the organisational framework for the first big intergovernmental Conference on the Movement of Persons from Central and Eastern European Countries held in Vienna on 24–25 January 1991. The conference was held on the initiative of the Austrian Ministry of Foreign Affairs, fearing an imminent mass migration following the collapse of the 'iron curtain', and gathered together the competent ministers of the member states of the Council of Europe plus several Central and Eastern European countries, the United States, Australia and Canada. The opening speech, given by the Secretary General of the Council of Europe, Catherine Lalumière, reflects the point of view of this institution and criticises the lack of solidarity in EU member states' efforts to control immigration to their territories: 'The five Schengen countries and the twelve Community countries run the danger of embarking on policies which are admirably co-ordinated, but co-ordinated only among themselves, leaving non-members of the "club" out in the cold.' (Council of Europe 1991a: 2).

The recommendations adopted by the conference reflect an unusual mixture of normative declarations on commitment to human rights, calls for measures to counter the abuse of asylum procedures, and statements on the issues of labour migration, the integration of legal immigrants, and the need for economic co-operation. In the final communiqué, the participants agreed to consider acceding to international instruments covering human rights and refugee principles and recommend the importance of international solidarity as basis of a harmonisation of immigration policies; to call for the harmonisation of asylum policies in order to prevent multiple asylum requests and for common visa and control policies at the borders; to recommend the introduction of temporary programmes for labour and student immigration; and to call for the fight against illegal labour. They also stressed the need for a co-operative policy of economic development towards the countries of emigration (Council of Europe 1991b: 7).

After this conference, co-operation amongst the Ministers of the Interior once again, as in the case of intergovernmental co-operation among EU member states in the 1980s, shifted from the humanitarian framework of the Council of Europe to an intergovernmental level in the Budapest Group.

As a consequence of this shift, the Committee of Ministers of the Council of Europe decided that its specialised committees, the CDMG and CAHAR, should meet once a year with the additional members of the Vienna Group and elaborate policies relating to pan-European migration (Conseil de l'Europe 1996). According to its mandate the CDMG concentrates on a wide range of migration issues such as the integration of legal immigrants, short-term migration programmes and the fight against racism and xenophobia. In contrast, CAHAR deals explicitly with asylum seekers and refugee law. Since it consists of EU member states, the associated CEECs and other European countries, CAHAR has become an important forum for deliberation amongst these different groups. In the early 1990s the new Central and Eastern European members did not really participate in these discussions, but their attitude changed when they were faced with the problem of refugees and asylum seekers and their incorporation into the European refugee regime. While their initial interest in CAHAR has been to use it as a forum for information and exchange regarding Western European policies, they have started to introduce sensitive issues into the discussion, such as the concept of 'safe third countries' at the behest of Hungary. In these deliberations, the fundamental divergence of interests between West and East, and between the EU and the Council of Europe became apparent: while both the humanitarian orientation of the Council of Europe and the geographical position of the CEECs as front-line countries supported the formulation of less strict guidelines for the application of the 'safe third country' notion, these guidelines were vetoed by the EU member states who had already agreed on more restrictive standards in the (non-binding) 1992 London Resolution.

THE BUDAPEST PROCESS

The Budapest process refers to the continuation of the inter-governmental negotiations started in the wake of the Vienna conference. The follow-up conference to Vienna was initiated by the German government and took place in Berlin on 30–31 October 1991. This Conference on Illegal Immigration from and through Central and Eastern Europe was attended by the Ministers of the Interior of the twelve EU countries, Switzerland, Austria and thirteen Central and East European governments, including Albania, the newly independent Baltic republics and Ukraine. The final communiqué of the conference expresses the fear of the West of losing control of 'the ever-increasing magnitude of the streams of migration from and through the countries of Eastern and Central Europe into the territories of the Western European countries' which would constitute a 'destabilising factor in all countries and place a burden on the harmonious development of relations between European peoples'. Accordingly, a number of tough co-ordinated measures to combat illegal immigration were adopted, including the imposition of severe penalties for the organised smuggling of clandestine immigrants; harmonised standards and rules of border controls; mobile forces to be deployed in remote frontier areas, and heavy sanctions against airlines which fail to check the travel documents of passengers at the point of departure. Furthermore, the harmonisation of visa policies and a general exchange process of information technology and intelligence information as well as the training of border guards were agreed.

The so-called Berlin Group was subsequently formed to follow the implementation of these recommendations. Compared to the declarations of Vienna, the focus of attention made a clear shift away from the question of human rights and international solidarity to an emphasis on prevention and control.

The follow-up conference was held on 15–16 February 1993 in Budapest and adopted a series of recommendations elaborated by the Berlin Group on how to tackle the problem of clandestine immigration. These recommendations cover the mutual assistance in criminal matters for the prosecution of smuggling of illegal immigrants; the setting up of special units and services to combat the activities of illegal migration networks; exchange of information on illegal migration; procedures and standards for the improvement of control at the border; surveillance of external borders which are not part of the authorised crossing points; sanctions against carriers transporting clandestine immigrants and technical and financial assistance to Central and Eastern European states. Another important topic of discussion was the conclusion of readmission agreements.

These discussions were pursued by the newly created Budapest Group, consisting of the states assuming the presidencies of the EU, the Schengen group and EFTA together with the Czech Republic, Poland, Slovakia and Hungary under the presidency of Hungary. In particular, the elaboration of a multilateral readmission agreement was proposed, but failed mainly due to Germany's preference of swifter and more flexible bilateral agreements.

The next conference of the Budapest Group took place in Prague on 14–15 October 1997. Here, several problematic issues were proposed such as the adoption of a principle according to which participating states should as far as possible return illegal aliens directly to their country of origin, the linkage of visa-free agreements with readmission agreements, and the fight against migrant trafficking as an increasingly significant form of 'organised international crime'.[21] This last point was the focal issue in following Budapest meeting in July 1998, organised on the initiative of Germany in order to adopt measures to tighten immigration controls throughout Europe in the fight against illegal immigration. The central idea behind the emerging co-operation in the context of the Budapest process is that the Southern and Eastern European countries should help the West in preventing illegal immigrants from reaching their territories, while the West in turn provides these countries with training and technology.

The Budapest process, although focusing on illegal immigration and not dealing explicitly with the issue of asylum seekers, is a major instrument in the dissemination of restrictive policies throughout Europe. With the publicity that it has gained, we can also observe an increasing–albeit rhetorical–awareness of the effects of the propagated measures on genuine refugees seeking asylum in Europe. A first indication of this is the inclusion of safeguards for asylum seekers in the final version of the declaration adopted at the last meeting in Budapest.

To summarise, an examination of the various bilateral and multilateral activities involving individual states, international organisations and other intergovernmental forums dealing with asylum and immigration matters generate a confusing image of overlapping and sometimes contradictory processes and diverging dynamics. Roughly, one can distinguish two different approaches to the role of Central and Eastern European countries in the European refugee regime which are supported by different actors. The dominant approach is promoted by Western European countries in unilateral, bilateral and multilateral processes to combat illegal immigration and large-scale refugee flows to their territories, with measures to ensure the implementation and export of restrictive policies. On the other hand, a multitude of international organisations, NGOs and other forums such as the Council of Europe stress the humanitarian dimension of the refugee problem and the need to admit refugees and to grant protection in accordance with the traditional values of the international refugee regime and human rights.

How can we explain the success of Western states in exporting a restrictive refugee regime, in which the CEECs play the role of front-line states protecting the West from undesired aliens? This apparent paradox has a political explanation. It is a function of the specific political context, that is, the question of European integration and the prospect of future membership in the European Union.

THE POLITICAL FRAME: ASYLUM, IMMIGRATION AND EU MEMBERSHIP

With the ongoing dynamics of integration, the issues of asylum and immigration have gained a genuinely European dimension in so far as they have been introduced into the external relations of the Union and now figure amongst the general requirements for accession to the EU. While the EU's external relations were originally based on purely economic considerations, the changes in Central and Eastern Europe have induced the introduction of a 'new conditionality' (Weber 1995: 189) in foreign policy which places increasing pressure on the political requirements for economic co-operation. With the confirmation of a future Eastern enlargement of the Union, these political criteria have steadily extended. Originally, political conditionality was limited to general requirements, such as the existence of stable democratic systems, the rule of law and respect for human rights, but it has gradually been extended to include the totality of formal and informal regulations on justice and home affairs adopted under the Maastricht Treaty and within the framework of Schengen. While political criteria were initially separated from the question of EU membership, they were nevertheless almost directly linked to the strategies of pre-adhesion. In the meantime, all CEECs have applied for EU membership,[22] and adaptation to the 'acquis' reached under the political pillars of the Union is no longer a problem of national interests or intergovernmental relations, but an indispensable step in their efforts to become member states.

The next section formulates two arguments in relation to the co-operation processes occurring in the context of a future enlargement of the European Union. Firstly, far from being a well-defined and clear objective, the conditions for membership presented to the CEECs have been progressively extended and include an increasing number of measures which exceed the scope of obligations for the actual member states of the Union.

Secondly, this steady extension is less a result of the progressive integration into the contemporary EU, for example, through a deepening of its 'acquis' than it is a requirement of the member states' interests and their ambiguous and, at times, protectionist attitude towards Eastern enlargement.

The Politics of Enlargement: The Institutional Framework

Since the collapse of Communism, the EU has gradually intensified its relations with the countries of Central and Eastern Europe. Starting from the collapse of Communism in 1989, one can distinguish three phases of co-operation between the EU and the CEECs: a first phase of rather uncommitted economic relations between 1989 and 1993; a second phase of preparation for enlargement designed to bring the CEEC's in line with the core provisions of the EU single market from 1993 to 1997; and a third phase of intensified negotiations entailing both a clarification of the 'acquis' to be adopted by applicant countries in order to join, and the implementation of formal procedures for the evaluation of the CEECs' qualification for accession.[23]

In the period immediately following 1989, the EU was slow to clarify its relationship with the newly democratising countries of Central and Eastern Europe. This first phase of EU-CEEC relations was mainly based on the conclusion of rather limited trade and co-operation agreements (Sedelmeier 1994; Sedelmeier and Wallace 1996). A second important instrument adopted in this period is the PHARE programme established in 1990 to provide aid and technical assistance to support the process of economic restructuring and transition.[24] During the first phase of EU-CEEC relations, this aid programme included financial support for economic transformation and the establishment of a market-oriented economy, designed to promote private enterprise and help consolidate democracy. PHARE was originally limited to Poland and Hungary, but was subsequently extended to cover all ten applicants for membership together with Albania, Bosnia-Herzegovina and the Former Yugoslav Republic of Macedonia (Croatia's participation is currently suspended).

The second phase in EU-CEEC relations started with the conclusion of more comprehensive 'Europe Agreements' with Hungary and Poland (1991), the Czech Republic, Romania, Bulgaria (1993), Slovakia and the Baltic states (1995), and Slovenia (1996). These agreements started the process of approximating the CEECs to the Union's 'acquis' by gradually extending the four freedoms of the single market (the free movement of goods, services, capital and labour) to these countries over a ten-year period. The agreements, originally independent of the question of EU membership, were subsequently linked to a number of political conditionalities and subsequently became a central instrument in the EU's pre-accession strategy. The decision to link these agreements with EU enlargement was made at the European Council meeting in Copenhagen in June 1993, where the EU governments decided that countries signing such agreements would be eligible for EU membership. At the Copenhagen European Council, the following general conditions were laid down for membership:

- the stability of institutions guaranteeing democracy, the rule of law, human rights and respect for, and the protection of, minorities;
- the existence of a functioning market economy, together with the capacity to cope with competitive pressure and market forces within the Union;
- the ability to take on the obligations of membership, including adherence to the aims of political, economic, and monetary union;
- and finally, the capacity on the part of the Union to absorb new members, while maintaining the momentum of European integration.

This official 'pre-accession strategy' was formally launched one year after the adoption of these general guidelines at the Essen European Council in December 1994. The strategy incorporated the general framework for adapting to EU requirements set down in the Europe Agreements and the PHARE programme and sup-plemented these with the Single Market White Paper and the Structured Dialogue. The Single Market White Paper is a non-binding document elaborated by the European Commission set-ting out the key legislation governing trade in goods and services in the EU's internal market. Although designed originally as a document for guidance rather than as a legal framework of EU-CEEC relations, the White Paper has become a key element in the EU's pre-accession strategy, since it provides the basis on which the Commission will assess the ability of the candidate countries to take on the obligations of membership (Grabbe 1998). By contrast, the Structured Dialogue was set up as a multi-lateral forum for discussion between the EU institutions, the member states and the CEECs, to give a broader framework to bilateral consultations in the Europe Agreements and to provide a new impetus for the association process.

By summer 1997, dissatisfaction with the functioning of this framework of co-operation brought an end to this second phase of EU-CEEC relations. Official criticism focused on the fact that failure to establish a clear strategy for enlargement meant that the adopted measures were limited to the stipulation of specific requirements in selected policy fields without establishing a comprehensive plan for accession. In particular, the Structured Dialogue proved inefficient given the absence of any clear and substantial focus and the lack of decision-making powers.[25] Apart from these official reproaches, both academics and rep-resentatives of the CEECs have criticised this second phase of pre-accession strategies for the asymmetrical distribution of power between a dominant EU and the weaker CEECs, an in-sufficient involvement and information of the applicant coun-tries, and a bias towards neo-liberal economic policies which may run counter to the needs of the transitional economies of the CEECs.[26]

The third and current phase of EU-CEEC relations was launched with the publication of the Commission's 'avis' (or opinions) on the applicants' progress in meeting the Copenha-gen conditions and the proposal for a new 'reinforced' pre-accession strategy in its Agenda 2000. The Commission's 'avis' on the ten applicant countries give a synopsis of the applicants' readiness for membership based on an overview of the political and economic situation in each country.[27] The basis for these evaluations is the conditions for membership set down at the Council meeting in Copenhagen. As a conclusion, the Commission proposed to start accession negotiations with Hungary, Poland, Estonia, the Czech Republic and Slovenia in 1998. The first accessions should take place between 2001 and 2003 (EC Commission 1997b). With this proposal, later approved by the Council, the EU formally adopted a differentiated approach towards CEE applicants and opted for an enlargement in stages.

The new framework for co-operation with the CEECs proposed in Agenda 2000 is the 'Accession Partnerships'. These set up a common structure for all applicants, irrespective of whether they are already engaged in negotiations, and set priorities for adaptation to the EU 'acquis' on a timetable of short and medium-term priorities for each applicant. The basis for these priorities are the 'avis' established by the Commission, annual reports by the Commission on the candidates' progress and the CEECs' own 'National Programmes for Adoption of the Acquis' in which they set timetables for achieving the priorities. With the Accession Partnerships, the range of policies to be adopted by the candidate countries is constantly being redefined. This not only clarifies the still very equivocal conditions for membership, but also generates the gradual extension of these conditions which also tend to cover issues which are not formally binding for the present EU member states.[28]

With the restructuring of pre-accession relations, the Commission has carried through a reform of the financial framework of co-operation. The PHARE programme has been re-organised to be directly targeted on the objectives set out in the Accession Partnership agreements and has thus moved from a demand-driven philosophy, based on the needs expressed by the candidate countries, to an accession-driven approach conceived to meet the Union requirements for membership. Given the dissatisfaction with the earlier output of PHARE programmes, the

Commission intends to apply strict conditionality for financial support directly linked to each country's success in meeting the objectives set out in its partnership agreements. From the year 2000 onwards, additional financial support will be available from the EU Structural Funds.

In the meantime, a first round of accession negotiations started in March 1998 with the Czech Republic, Estonia, Hungary, Poland and Slovenia. Since the beginning of accession talks in 1993, the conditions for EU enlargement have gradually been clarified, leading to a constant expansion of the 'acquis' to be adopted before joining the Union. This expansion is particularly salient in the policy fields pertaining to the former third pillar of the Maastricht Treaty on justice and home affairs. These hitherto intergovernmental fields of co-operation, although originally excluded from the official EU-CEEC relations, have now moved to the centre stage in negotiations and may well become a major obstacle to future enlargement.

Asylum and Immigration: Conditions for Membership

The policy fields of asylum and immigration, which are now important conditions for EU membership, entered the official policies of enlargement relatively late. Several considerations have contributed to this delay. On the one hand, this may be due to the intergovernmental nature of these policy fields and member states' concern with retaining sovereignty in these matters. An official introduction of intergovernmental agreements on the agenda for enlargement could be perceived as a formalisation of hitherto loose arrangements, thereby strengthening their binding effect within the Union itself. Furthermore, the inclusion of these policy fields in the requirements for membership would eventually lead to an increased competence of the Commission in these matters, a development which the member states have always fiercely opposed. On the other hand, this reluctance to officially include these matters in the EU's relations with the

CEECs relied on the fact that at the bilateral level, the extension of restrictive measures against illegal immigration and for the redistribution of asylum seekers had already materialised, making their formal 'Europeanisation' obsolete. Moreover, these bilateral consultations allowed the member states to focus intervention according to their geographical interests and allowed a high degree of informality and speed.

Apart from the strong protectionism of member states' governments against co-operation in asylum and immigration matters, the obscure legal nature of the agreements taken under the third pillar–informal and non-binding instruments–also contributes to the confusion as to the scope of the 'acquis' reached in this field. Finally, the Commission may itself be reluctant to introduce these matters into its foreign relations. In contrast to the earlier 'political conditionality' implied in foreign policy instruments such as the PHARE programme and Co-operation and Association Agreements that gave equal billing to political liberalisation–human rights, democracy, civic freedoms–and the economic liberalisation of markets, trade, and investment regimes, the issues of asylum and immigration do not refer to the fundamental freedoms of own citizens but touch the respective countries' external relations and their policies towards aliens.

The introduction of political co-operation with regard to justice and home affairs in the pre-accession strategy was supported, together with co-operation in foreign and security policy, by a 1993 initiative of the British and Italian Ministers for Foreign Affairs, Douglas Hurd and Beniamino Andreatta, which called for a strengthening of the political dialogue with the CEECs. This was confirmed at the European Council meeting in Essen in December 1994. Here, the heads of government agreed on a pre-accession strategy for the gradual approximation of the associated countries to the Union. Since then, these matters have become an official part of the relations between the EU and the associated countries. Co-operation has been promoted both by the supranational institutions (the Commission and the Parliament) and the Council using all three pre-accession instruments: the Europe Agreements, the Structured Dialogue, and the PHARE programme. In addition, several initiatives have been launched by the European Commission under Title VI of the European Union Treaty on Justice and Home Affairs. With the new phase of pre-accession strategies launched in 1997, asylum and immigration matters have increasingly moved to the centre of EU-CEEC relations.

THE EUROPE AGREEMENTS

The Europe Association Agreements were originally limited to trade and economic co-operation, but with the Copenhagen European Council, they acquired a political dimension and a regular political dialogue of their own. A key element was the Association Councils, a series of twice-yearly bilateral meetings between the EU and each of the partner countries. Although the agreements did not explicitly contain a clause mentioning asylum or immigration as such, their Association Councils and Committee meetings were used as forums where this subject could be discussed between individual CEECs and the EU as a whole as represented by the Commission and the Presidency or the Council (European Commission 1997a: 33). However, these policy fields were not much discussed in this framework due to their intergovernmental nature.

THE STRUCTURED DIALOGUE

The Structured Dialogue was established parallel to the bilateral system of co-operation in the Europe Agreements as a forum for multilateral consultations in various policy fields. Originally intended to develop in a series of regular meetings between the EU institutions and the associated countries, it is generally perceived as having contributed little to the enlargement strategies.

Taking note of the multiplicity of both bilateral and mutlilateral intergovernmental consultations in matters relating to asylum and immigration between the member states and the CEECs which occurred outside the EU framework, in July 1994 the European Commission urged the Justice and Interior Ministers to take a decision on the procedures for consulting and informing the CEECs within a more structured, and hence formal, relationship in the fields of justice and home affairs. Up until this point, the emphasis had been limited to subjects related to the battle against organised crime, including the strengthening of borders and the fight against illegal immigration, whilst sidestepping the issue of closer co-operation in asylum-related matters. Here, the establishment of adequate procedures and standards would be in the interests of both partners and an essential preparation for eventual membership of the Union (EC Commission 1994b: 3). This appeal can be interpreted as an indication that the extension of the system of redistribution of asylum seekers based on the 'safe third country' rule required the implementation of certain legal, administrative and institutional standards of refugee protection in the CEECs.

Soon after this appeal, the heads of government decided at the Essen European Council to give the issues of the third pillar, including asylum, more weight in the Structured Dialogue and to integrate co-operation in asylum and immigration matters in the pre-accession strategy. This, however, proved relatively ineffective. Between the Essen Council and summer 1997, the EU Ministers of Justice and Home Affairs only met their Central and Eastern European counterparts twice. The first meeting was the informal Ministerial Conference on Drugs and Organised Crime held in Berlin in September 1994. This was the first time that the Ministers of Justice and Home Affairs from the CEECs were invited to meet their EU, and some other European, counterparts. The common declaration adopted at the conference emphasises the need for co-operation both with regard to the prospect of accession of the associated countries to the EU and to the new challenges emerging in Europe. In particular, it sets out the priorities in the field of justice and home affairs which reflect the interests of the EU member states *vis-à-vis* their Central and Eastern European counterparts. According to these priorities, co-operation should focus on combating serious forms of crime, including traffic in human beings and illegal immigration networks (Council of the European Union General Secretariat 1994: 6).

With regard to the latter, it was agreed to improve co-operation in visa policy; effective border controls and border surveillance; effective sanctions against sea and air carriers; the introduction of provisions that penalise the illegal smuggling of aliens, and the rapid return of illegal aliens to their countries of origin. To this end, several concrete measures were considered, such as the exchange of liaison officers and experts for the transfer of expertise, technology and training. These issues continued to represent the focus of activities in the Structured Dialogue with the Council of Justice and Home Affairs in the following two years.

Although bilateral and unilateral activities in asylum matters had already been put forward for several years by EU member states and in the framework of the third pillar, it was only in 1997 that asylum and immigration were given priority in the Structured Dialogue with the Council. For a long time, the contents of the Union's legal 'acquis' in these fields was blurred between binding intergovernmental conventions, non-binding resolutions and declamatory conclusions, but an informal determination of its contents was made in 1996 with a letter from the Irish Presidency to the CEECs. In this letter, practically all instruments adopted by the EU member states before and after the entry into force of the Maastricht Treaty are included, together with the formally non-binding resolutions and conclusions. Although this letter does not represent a formal determination of the 'acquis' in the field, it nevertheless strengthens the legal status of these provisions since it makes their domestic implementation compulsory on the CEECs in their efforts to join the Union.

Following the letter, the first and, to date, the only expert meeting with representatives of the CEECs took place in the asylum working group in February 1997. Given the brevity of the meeting, the discussion remained general and focused on the state of legal adaptation in the associated countries.

On 27 May 1997, a second meeting of the Justice and Home Affairs Council bringing together ministers from the EU and the associated countries took place in Brussels. Here, the representatives of the respective CEECs were able to comment on the perception of the co-operation in asylum and immigration matters. The main points of discussion were the 'safe third country' rule, the possibility of applying the Parallel Dublin Convention and the integration of refugees into society. On this occasion, several countries expressed their concern with being swamped by asylum seekers returned by EU countries on grounds of the 'safe third country' rule. In order to compensate for these eventualities, the CEECs proposed to differentiate between front-line countries, directly exposed to refugee flows, and centre countries, protected by the 'safe third country' notion in the emerging pan-European refugee regime. These protected centre countries, which, given their relative wealth, would be the favoured destination of many migrants and refugees, would be requested to provide the front-line countries, in this case the CEECs themselves, with financial support. In addition to this critical proposal, the CEECs were dissatisfied with the practice of the Structured Dialogue and the low level of participation accorded to them in these matters. In fact, the Structured Dialogue turned out to be less a forum for mutual exchange and co-operation than a very limited series of special meetings outside the normal work of the Council. Contrary to earlier expectations, the CEECs have neither been accepted as observers in the regular meetings, nor have they been informed about ongoing negotiations. Without this information, they had no chance to exert influence on co-operation amongst EU member states and are merely informed *ex post* of official decisions.

THE ACCESSION PARTNERSHIPS

It is not clear how far the newly launched Accession Partnerships will change the asymmetric nature of accession talks, and observers of the pre-accession process hint at an increasing dominance of EU institutions in the determination of accession conditions and a significant reduction of the margins for negotiations in comparison to earlier enlargements (Grabbe 1998).

The first step towards a formal determination of the 'acquis' adopted in the third pillar on justice and home affairs was made with the Commission's 'avis', where these provisions are subsumed under the ability to assume the obligations of membership. The obligations of candidates in this field are very broad, since they include not only the formal conventions and other instruments adopted by the member states, but also informal and non-binding ones such as resolutions and conclusions and also 'the agreed elements of draft instruments which are in negotiation' (EC Commission 1997b: B.3.7). Furthermore, the 'acquis' is not limited to these formal, informal, and uncompleted instruments adopted in the EU framework, but also includes all the provisions of the Schengen Agreement plus the–mostly unpublished–decisions taken by the executive committee of Schengen since 1990. It can be assumed that the introduction of Schengen into the EU framework with the Amsterdam Treaty was–at least partly–intended to provide a legal basis for these expansive obligations to applicant countries. This assumption is supported by the new Article 49 of the TEU, which provides that every European state which wants to become a member of the EU must introduce the full 'acquis' in its national laws. With the progress of accession negotiations, the adoption of the Schengen 'acquis', which relates mostly to the strengthening of external borders, the fight against illegal immigration has become a priority for all candidate countries. At a meeting with EU Ministers of the Interior in June 1998, the CEECs agreed to gradually introduce the Schengen 'acquis' even before their accession to the EU and put it into practice. At the same meeting, the Schengen states stressed that accession to the EU will not take place before the CEECs have implemented tight and efficient border control measures.[29] In order to stress this commitment, the EU and applicant countries signed a 'Pre-accession Pact against Organised Crime' in May 1998 to support the CEECs' adoption of the 'acquis' in justice and home affairs and to develop and implement joint projects against organised crime, including trafficking in human beings and 'organised illegal immigration'.[30] This emphasis on the justice and home affairs 'acquis' in relation with the CEECs contrasts sharply with the, to date, weak and legally non-binding nature of member states' own obligations in these fields, reflected not only in the use of soft law, but also in the extensive opt-outs negotiated in the Amsterdam Treaty.

On the basis of these enlarged membership conditions, the 'avis' given by the Commission in the fields of justice and home affairs cover a broad range of issues. As general conditions, they include the accession of the CEECs to relevant international treaties, the observation of the rule of law, the stability of administrative and judicial institutions, and data protection. With regard to specific policy fields, they assess the establishment of equitable asylum procedures and laws as well as the adoption of restrictive measures to limit immigration and to ensure stringent border controls. They focus, in particular, on the tightening up of visa regimes; the strengthening of admission systems, for example with regard to restrictive rules on residence and work permits or naturalisation; the tightening up of enforcement and deportation procedures; the introduction of penalties for illegal immigration, and the adoption of sanctions against carriers enabling the illegal entry of foreigners; the conclusion of readmission agreements with Western and other Central, Eastern, and Southern European countries; and finally the reform of the border management systems improving control and surveillance mechanisms.[31]

Unlike the broader framework of enlargement processes, where the Commission is competent to evaluate the CEECs' preparations, the screening of their progress in justice and home affairs will be assessed by a governmental body composed of governmental representatives of the EU member states. In April 1998, the Council of Ministers set up a group of experts to evaluate the enactment, application and effective implementation by the applicant countries of the EU 'acquis' in these fields. This expert group operates under the supervision of a political body, namely the Committee of Permanent Representatives of the Member States (COREPER). It makes an evaluation on the basis of information provided by the member states in their bilateral and multilateral activities with the CEECs and the member states' embassies in these countries as well as European Commission delegations, the European Commission through its role in the overall process of accession and the PHARE programme, and reports made by the Council of Europe on the implementation of the relevant conventions and recommendations. With these exceptional proceedings, the member states have once again asserted their sovereignty over the policy fields pertaining to justice and home affairs.

THE PHARE PROGRAMME

The extension of the PHARE programme to justice and home affairs was prepared by an independent expert employed by the European Commission, Anthony Langdon, who was responsible for producing a report on the situation of justice and home affairs in the CEECs. After visiting each of the associated countries, in 1995 Langdon submitted the so-called 'Langdon Report' which sets the priorities for co-operation in these areas and makes propositions for the allocation of PHARE assistance. The report calls for the adoption of measures to combat illegal immigration and to enforce border controls, the need to build up the institutions and procedures necessary for a working and well-informed asylum system, and the need to combat drug trafficking.

Since then the Commission has engaged in a series of bilateral discussions with each associated CEEC to identify the specific needs for which PHARE funds might be used. Several programmes relating to asylum and immigration have been launched. Given the priority placed on the question of effective immigration control, the initial focus has been on the enforcement of the Eastern borders. The Baltic Eastern Border Management Programme has been set up to help Latvia, Lithuania and Estonia improve the level and management of control of their eastern borders. In Poland, support has been granted for border guards at the eastern border. In addition, a comprehensive programme was developed to cover the issues of migration and asylum to promote the development of a legal and institutional framework for immigration and asylum and to enhance the capabilities of the border guards to carry out effective border management and to tackle illegal activities.

As with the generally negative assessment of progress regarding the allocation of PHARE funds, satisfaction with the results reached in the fields of justice and home affairs was limited. With the re-organisation of PHARE into an accession-driven instrument, its focus will be geared to the fulfilment of membership conditions as assessed in the Commission's 'avis'. In this context a multilateral PHARE Justice and Home Affairs horizontal programme, which places the emphasis on interregional co-operation and multi-country activities, especially in the field of training, information provision and exchange, has been launched. Whereas previously, PHARE money had been allocated to the CEECs when they applied for funds, the new programmes can now be proposed by EU member states, the European Commission and other institutions such as the Council of Europe or the UNHCR. This overarching programme is intended to be a complement particularly in areas of interest to the EU which are not accorded sufficient importance in the national programmes. The co-operation includes legal, administrative and operational aspects. According to the priorities set by the EU Commission in the accession partnership, in the field of justice and home affairs PHARE funding for all ten CEECs should concentrate on the development of effective border management and in the medium term on the establishment of asylum systems and related measures.[32] With regard to the latter, the Commission would preferentially support the development of adequate institutional frameworks for dealing with refugees and asylum seekers, the implementation of asylum procedures, including the training of personnel and the development of documentary and information sources. Furthermore, PHARE should also support the development of legal advisory systems and NGOs dealing with refugees. These activities could be accompanied by research, seminars and other exchanges dealing with refugees and specific elements of the 'acquis' or other common practical issues (EC Commission 1997a: 32–33).

OTHER EU ACTIVITIES

In addition to these official instruments of the pre-accession strategy, exchange in asylum and immigration matters has also been promoted by other EU initiatives. Seminars on asylum law in the European Union were organised by the European Commission financed by the budget of the third pillar of the Maastricht Treaty. The participants were officials from several Central and Eastern European countries dealing with asylum procedures and experts from a number of EU member states. In addition, the Commission launched an overarching co-operation programme called 'Odysseus' to promote the exchange of public officials from both member and associated countries who are working in the fields of asylum, immigration and border enforcement. In June 1998, money from the Odysseus programme was used to finance the meeting of the Budapest Group. This indicates that the Commission is increasingly willing to accept the dominant role of intergovernmental consultations in the enlargement of justice and home affairs.

Another important initiative was taken by the Committee for Civil Liberties and Internal Affairs of the European Parliament, which held a series of joint meetings with the responsible parliamentary committees of the ten associated countries in Central and Eastern Europe to discuss the problems of organised crime, migration and asylum. The underlying rationale of this co-operation is the realisation that asylum and immigration policies could no longer be considered from an exclusively national point of view, nor that of the European Union alone, but had to take account of the Eastern neighbours. It was recognised that EU policies had reciprocal effects: tighter border controls and changes in visa policy discouraged illegal immigration into EU countries and conversely, if the EU decided that asylum seekers could be sent to CEECs on the grounds of the 'safe third country' rule, the number of asylum seekers in these countries would substantially increase (EP 1997: 5).

CONCLUSION

With the progress of enlargement discussions between the EU and the CEECs, the obligations on candidate countries for membership were progressively expanded from general political requirements with regard to the stability of democratic and liberal regimes and economic conditions to the fields of justice and home affairs, which are only slowly becoming fully communitarised in the EU structure. Although asylum and immigration issues were only placed on the EU's CEEC agenda relatively late on, co-operation in these matters was already well developed at the bilateral and multilateral levels and was predominantly promoted by single member states fearing an increase of immigration from, and through, these countries. With the prospect of EU enlargement, these mainly bilateral and intergovernmental processes have acquired a genuine European dimension and a political legitimisation as conditions for membership of the European Union.

Co-operation with the CEECs induced by Western concerns to combat illegal immigration and to reduce the numbers of asylum seekers on their territory has mainly focused on the export of restrictive policies and has largely been dictated by member states' policies such as the adoption of the 'safe third country' rule, the conclusion of readmission agreements and the enforcement of border controls. These measures, supported by intergovernmental forums such as the Justice and Home Affairs Council or the Budapest Group, have effectively extended the system of redistribution for handling asylum claims which is the key element of the EU refugee regime. In the light of the restrictions of asylum and immigration policies in the West, this causes increasing numbers of asylum seekers, refugees and immigrants to remain in the CEECs, and the rapid adaptation of the latter to the protectionist policies of the EU member states.

Faced with these developments, a multitude of international organisations and NGOs have mobilised in order to counterbalance this restrictive trend by emphasising the need to safeguard basic international human rights norms and the rule of law. Their efforts concentrate on the prevention of involuntary migration, the implementation of basic legislative provisions and the establishment of an administrative and organisational infrastructure for the protection of refugees.

Against this background, the enlargement of EU asylum and immigration policies *vis-à-vis* the CEECs faces several challenges. Firstly, the multitude of bilateral and multilateral processes surrounding the introduction of asylum and immigration matters in the CEECs poses a problem of *co-ordination* for the European Commission in view of a future enlargement. This problem in turn has several dimensions. Firstly, the existence of multiple actors entails a lack of information and transparency with regard to the activities pursued in the field and the risk of overlaps. Secondly, the challenge of co-ordination is enhanced by the, at times, contradictory logics guiding these endeavours— the protectionist policies promoted by the member states in view of safeguarding internal security which focus mainly on the sealing of the Eastern borders on the one hand, and the need to respect basic humanitarian standards towards asylum seekers, refugees and immigrants expressed predominantly by international organisations and NGOs on the other. This is supported by the fact that member states' policies follow clearly regional interests, the most active being the Scandinavian countries *vis-à-vis* the Baltic states and Germany *vis-à-vis* its neighbours.

The second challenge derives from the intergovernmental nature of the third pillar on justice and home affairs which gives the member states an unprecedented degree of sovereignty and autonomy in the relations with the CEECs and raises the problem of EC *competence* in these matters. This problem is supported by the very sensitive nature of the policy fields of the third pillar as core issues of national sovereignty. Thus, the Commission will have to find more indirect ways of tackling existing needs in the fields of asylum and immigration, for instance through the provision of systematic PHARE programmes or the organisation of expert seminars as in the Odysseus programme. This problem will not be fully resolved when the issues of asylum and immigration matters move to the first pillar. Not only will the member states try to maintain control over these matters, but supranational action will be hampered by the many interdependencies between asylum, immigration and questions of border controls or police co-operation in the fight against human smuggling which remain subject to intergovernmental co-operation.

Another difficulty arising from enlarging the third pillar 'acquis' to Central and Eastern Europe is its inherent tension with the provision for the *free movement of persons,* which is an integral part of the Single Market Programme. This tension has a long history, since co-operation in justice and home affairs began as a counter-reaction to the confirmation of the aim to abolish internal border controls in Schengen and in 1993 in the Union. The enforcement of the external border and the tightening of immigration and asylum regulations are conceived as compensation measures necessary to safeguard internal security in the internal market. Similarly, fearing large-scale immigration from, and through, the CEECs, member states will insist on the implementation of high standards of border security and immigration control in these countries. Thus, their full adoption of the third pillar 'acquis' may well be used as a pretext for postponing the free movement of labour and of persons in general.

This challenge to the free movement of persons is aggravated by the prospect of an *enlargement in stages.* The emphasis on external borders and strict immigration policies may lead to tension in the relations between the CEECs and threaten historical and cultural ties in the region. The introduction of restrictive visa policies, for example, has already proved problematic in these newly liberalised states which for half a century have suffered restrictions on the right to travel. Furthermore, the fact that the citizens of some associated countries such as Bulgaria and Romania require visas to enter the Union, while others do not is a major point of controversy in their relations with the EU. Finally, among the CEECs a major problem posed by the emphasis on external borders in an enlargement in stages concerns the presence of huge ethnic minorities spread over a number of neighbouring countries such as, for example, the Hungarians in Romania, Slovakia, Slovenia, Serbia and Ukraine.

Last but not least, the enlargement of the third pillar 'acquis' is a highly complex enterprise which presupposes the existence of basic legal standards, respect for humanitarian norms and the presence of legal and administrative institutions to safeguard their application. This consideration is related with the first point on the tension between the export of restrictive policies and the attempts of humanitarian NGOs and international organisations. The implementation of the third pillar 'acquis' requires the implementation of international treaties adopted in the framework of the Council of Europe and the United Nations as well as the existence of working institutions to safeguard the rule of law. Recognising the need to *conform to overarching international norms* and the significant deficits in the associated countries' legal and institutional frameworks, the establishment of basic legal, administrative and operational standards has become a priority in the Commission's enlargement programme. This is particularly important in the field of refugee policies which are governed by an international regime based on the 1951 Geneva Refugee Convention.

NOTES

1. In this book, the term 'Central and Eastern Europe' includes the countries associated with the EU. These are Poland, Hungary, the Czech Republic, Bulgaria, Romania, Slovenia, Slovakia, and the three Baltic states: Estonia, Latvia, and Lithuania. Effects of this extension of the European refugee regime on other states of Eastern or South-Eastern Europe will only be mentioned in particular cases.

2. The 'acquis' of the European Union is understood as the sum of those norms which govern member states' action in matters within the competence of the Union and which must be accepted by adhering states. These norms may be derived from binding or non-binding sources from within or outside the Union.

3. These findings on the domestic implementation of the 'safe third country' rule are based on a study issued by the Danish Refugee Council (1998).

4. For a discussion of the relationship between the 'safe third country' rule and the international refugee regime, see Chapter 5 of this book.

5. In Germany, such readmission agreements were concluded with, for instance, Sweden (1954), Denmark (1954), Norway (1955), Switzerland (1955), France (1960), Austria (1961), and the Benelux countries (1966).

6. For an overview, see the statistics of the Intergovernmental Consultations on Asylum and Migration Policy in Europe, North America, and Australia.

7. According to information of the European Parliament, the following countries of Central and Eastern Europe have been designated as safe countries of origin by the member states: Bulgaria, the Czech Republic, Estonia, Hungary, Latvia, Lithuania, Poland, Romania and Slovenia for Denmark; Bulgaria, the Czech Republic, Hungary, Poland, Romania, and the Slovak Republic for Germany; Bulgaria, the Czech Republic, Estonia, Hungary, Latvia, Lithuania, Poland, Romania, and the Slovak Republic for Finland; Bulgaria, Poland, and Romania for the UK; and Bulgaria, the Czech Republic, Hungary, Poland, Romania and the Slovak Republic for the Netherlands (EP 1997: 11).

8. For example, the Benelux countries with Slovenia and Romania, the Nordic countries especially with the Baltic states, and France with Croatia, the Czech Republic, Hungary, Romania and Slovenia. Data on these readmission agreements is taken from Intergovernmental Consultations, 'Working Paper on Readmission Agreements'. In addition, in summer 1994 France signed a highly sensitive confidential readmission agreement with Algeria, which is a major refugee-sending country. This agreement was not made public until its revelation by *Le Monde* on 22 October 1994 (*Migration New Sheet* November 1994, No. 140).

9. See Schieffer (1997) for detailed descriptions of these agreements.

10. In the negotiations leading to the conclusion of the German-Czech readmission agreement, the Czech Republic refused to adopt the new model agree-

ment and insisted on taking the illegal crossing of the common border as the basis for the allocation of responsibility, as was the case in the first generation of readmission agreements. Nevertheless, this agreement does include some elements of the new type, since it omits the requirement of a certain duration of stay in the requested country and imposes low proofs on the requesting party.

11. In Germany, the 'smuggling' of asylum seekers and other illegal immigrants was officially included in the category of organised crime with the passing of a new law to combat crime in 1994 (see Busch 1996b).

12. The formal agreements regulating German-Polish co-operation in this area are, apart from the multilateral readmission agreement with the Schengen countries of 29 March 1991, in force since 1 May 1991, in particular the convention on good neighbour relations and friendly co-operation ('*Vertrag über gute Nachbarschaft und freundschaftliche Zusammenarbeit*') of 17 June 1991; the informal agreement on the establishment of a governmental commission for regional co-operation at the border ('*Notenwechsel über die Einrichtung einer Regierungskommission für regionale und grenznahe Zusammenarbeit*') of 17 June 1991; the agreement on co-operation for the combat of organised crime ('*Abkommen über die Zusammenarbeit bei der Bekämpfung der organisierten Kriminalität*') of 6 November 1991, in force as of 14 August 1992; the bilateral readmission agreement of 7 May 1993, in force as of 1 June 1993; and finally the convention on the co-operation of police and border authorities in the border region ('*Staatsvertrag über die Zusammenarbeit der Polizeibehörden und der Grenzschutzbehörden in den Grenzgebieten*') of 5 April 1995 (not yet in force). In addition, several agreements are being prepared which shall allow the establishment of common investigation troops, task forces, commanding and executing offices; see Dietrich (1998).

13. This financial transfer was linked to the obligation for Poland to purchase German material, which contributes not only to the German economy but also to a further approximation of the technical requirements necessary for cross-border communication (Dietrich 1998).

14. See the section dealing with the 'Budapest process' in this chapter.

15. This is due to the fact that the relevant agreement on co-operation among border and police authorities is not yet in force.

16. Although no majority was found for a resolution, a large part of the European Parliament supported this report (EP 1995: 7).

17. Third Meeting of the Expert Group of the Budapest Group, Implementation of Readmission Agreements, Report on Theme 2, revised version prepared by the Czech Republic and ICG, Budapest, 15–16 June 1995. The main differences between this proposal and the EU specimen readmission agreement are the type of entry for third-country nationals which determines the responsibility to readmit, the provisions covering stateless persons, and the question as to which contracting party should carry out the escort during the transit of third-country nationals. In sum, the Czech proposal is closer to traditional readmis-

sion agreements, as it is based on the illegal crossing of the common border with the contracting party and not on the question as to whether or not residence in the territory of a contracting party is lawful.

18. Third Meeting of the Expert Group of the Budapest Group, Implementation of Readmission Agreements, Report on Theme 2, revised version prepared by the Czech Republic and ICG, Budapest, 15–16 June 1995.

19. See Peter Schatzer, Director of External Relations at IOM (Schatzer 1995).

20. Until 1995, the CSCE (Conference on Security and Co-operation in Europe).

21. Conference of Ministers on the Prevention of Illegal Migration held in the Context of the Budapest Process, Draft Recommendations of the meeting in Prague on 14–15 October 1997, version of 31 July 1997.

22. The dates of application are: Hungary in March 1994; Poland in April 1994; Romania and Slovakia in June 1995; Latvia in October 1995; Estonia in November 1995; Lithuania and Bulgaria in December 1995; the Czech Republic in January 1996; and Slovenia in June 1996.

23. For a detailed analysis of these three phases in EU-CEEC relations, see Grabbe (1998) and Grabbe and Hughes (1998).

24. 'PHARE' stands for 'Poland, Hungary Aid for Reconstruction' and was originally designed to support economic reforms of the sectors of agriculture, ecology, finance, industry, infrastructure, the social sector and education. A similar programme has been established for the newly independent states of the former Soviet Union called TACIS.

25. As a result, it has sometimes been referred to as the 'unstructured monologue'.

26. For a critical discussion of the pre-accession strategy, see Grabbe (1998) and Grabbe and Hughes 1998.

27. These 'avis' distinguish themselves from earlier EU enlargement in that they not only judge the applicants' readiness for membership now but rather take a medium-term view on whether they will be able to meet the requirements for membership within a time-span of five to ten years.

28. This point is discussed in Grabbe (1998).

29. *Uniting Europe* No. 13 of 29 June 1998.

30. *Uniting Europe* No. 4 of 27 April 1998, No. 10 of 8 June 1998.

31. The other policy fields covered in the 'avis' on justice and home affairs include police co-operation, drugs and judicial co-operation. A short assessment of the conclusions reached towards each CEEC in the 'avis' is given in the section on the CEECs' adaptation to the EU regime.

32. See the list of priorities in *Uniting Europe* No. 2 of 13 April 1998; No. 3 of 20 April 1998 and No. 4 of 27 April 1998. See also *European Report* No. 2326 of 24 June 1998.

4 Central and Eastern Europe's Adaptation to the EU 'Acquis'

With the transition to democracy, the associated countries of Central and Eastern Europe have progressively acceded to the fundamental treaties of the international refugee regime. While this move may be seen as an expression of their commitment to humanitarian and liberal values, such as the freedom of expression and the principle of non-discrimination, the preceding chapter has identified another dynamic underlying these processes, which originates in Western endeavours to combat illegal immigration and to limit incoming flows of asylum seekers. With the ongoing process of European integration, co-operation among EU member states in these matters has been gradually introduced onto the Union's agenda and now occupies a prominent place in EU-CEEC relations. In the context of Eastern enlargement, the CEECs' adaptation to the EU 'acquis' in this field and their preparedness to combat illegal immigration constitute key conditions for future accession.

With this formal introduction of mainly bilateral, purely inter-governmental and mostly informal activities *vis-à-vis* their Eastern neighbours, the EU has made the adoption of legislative, administrative and technological reforms in justice and home affairs a priority in the associated countries. Since the 1990s, we can observe the adhesion of the associated CEECs to the EU refugee regime through the adoption of key international treaties and the establishment of asylum systems. These processes are dictated not only by the desire to accede to the Union, but also as a direct reaction to increasing numbers of asylum seekers and refugees in these countries due to the increasing tightening up of Western borders and the unilateral designation of these countries as 'safe' by their Western neighbours coupled with the signing of bilateral and multilateral readmission agreements. Until recently, the CEECs perceived themselves as transit countries for foreigners heading West, whereas now they are rapidly becoming countries of *de facto* immigration. Immigrants and asylum seekers in Central and Eastern Europe mainly come from other Eastern European countries, but also from the Far East, the Middle East and Africa. Thus, spurred by Western endeavours to protect their territory from migration and refugee flows, the CEECs' gradual accession to the international refugee regime is influenced by the competing goals of satisfying international humanitarian standards as required by the West for the implementation of the 'safe third country' rule on the one hand, and the imperatives of control and the overarching objective of limiting immigration on the other.

The following country descriptions document the legislative adaptation of the CEECs to Western European asylum and immigration policies and demonstrate that, caught between the competing paradigms of protection and restriction, this adaptation leads to the proliferation of restrictive policies in the CEECs in order not to become a 'buffer zone' for asylum seekers and refugees heading towards Western Europe. Coupled with the primary aim of attaining Union membership, these adaptation processes turn into a sort of 'regulatory competition', in which each country seeks to be more restrictive than its neighbour in order not to increase its exposure to refugee flows. This, in turn, goes along with a further redistribution of asylum seekers and refugees east and south of the associated countries, thereby leading to the unrelenting expansion of EU policies to a pan-European refugee regime.

BULGARIA

Bulgaria was a relatively late entrant to the international refugee regime, and it is claimed that by mid-1991 national officials did not even have access to an official translation of the Geneva Convention (Engelbrekt 1994: 38). Nevertheless, the Convention and its 1967 Protocol were signed in 1992. The country has so far been mainly regarded as a transit country for migrants and refugees heading towards Western Europe. In November 1993, the Secretary General of the Ministry of Internal Affairs stated that the country was host to some 40,000 people whose goal was to reach Western Europe (Engelbrekt 1994: 37). Given its difficult economic situation, Bulgaria has so far accorded low priority to refugee issues compared with other socio-economic problems.

The wish to join the European Union seems to have been the major factor leading to Bulgarian adhesion to the international refugee regime. However, although the Geneva Convention and the New York Protocol were ratified in 1992, the Bulgarian asylum procedures continued to be regulated by a 1967 presidential edict for another two years. Subsequently, a National Bureau for Territorial, Asylum and Refugee Issues (NBTAR) was created and became operational in 1993 (EP 1997: 22; Engelbrekt 1994: 39). In 1994, a refugee law was drafted but, due to the lack of urgency attributed to this policy field, is not expected to enter into force in the near future (EP 1997: 3). In the meantime, the Bulgarian asylum system is governed by the general laws on aliens and the governmental decree on the establishment of NBTAR of October 1994.

The competent authority for the examination and decision-making on asylum claims is the Bureau on Territorial Asylum and Refugees. According to the administrative procedural law, an appeal against a negative decision may be lodged with the Higher Administrative Court, whose decision is final. In practice, the 'safe third country' rule is applied and precludes access to asylum procedures for asylum seekers who have travelled through such a country in transit before entering Bulgaria.

The Bulgarian asylum system has been much criticised for its lack of a consistent legal framework and the poor co-ordination between the ministries involved. The UNHCR has pointed out that potential asylum seekers are sometimes denied entry at border stations. This is partly due to the fact that officials authorised to receive asylum applications at border points are not permanently present. Moreover, since the border police are not issued with specific instructions on how to deal with asylum seekers nor trained in refugee law, those placed at the borders do not normally make a distinction between illegal immigrants and asylum seekers or refugees (Danish Refugee Council 1998).

In contrast to the relatively underdeveloped asylum system, Bulgaria has made considerable efforts to curb illegal immigration and to strengthen its borders, officially, as one of the prerequisites for accession to the European Union. The twofold aims of Bulgarian policy are to reduce the numbers of outgoing Bulgarian migrants heading towards Western Europe on the one hand, and to prevent further incoming flows of immigration from third-country nationals on the other. From 1994 onwards, readmission agreements were concluded with Poland, Switzerland, Germany, Slovakia, Greece, Spain, France, and Lithuania, and others are being negotiated with the Czech Republic, Slovenia, Croatia and Portugal (EP 1997: 21). In addition, in order to fight illegal immigration, the Ministry of the Interior has formulated a large-scale programme, partly financed by PHARE money, to tighten up its national borders (EP 1997: 23). In 1997, the responsibilities for controlling border crossings were transferred from the National Security Service to the National Border Guard Service, which will be gradually transformed into a border police. In this way, Bulgaria has set up an integrated system for border protection and passport and visa control at the state borders. The stepping up of immigration control has finally been complemented by a reform of visa policies. Bulgaria has placed restrictive visa requirements on nationals from the most important illegal immigrant exporting countries. The toughest restrictions apply to persons from the former Soviet republics, who need a formal invitation from a Bulgarian citizen or a document certifying that their visit is for business purposes in order to enter the country, and must bring a certain amount of money for their stay and a pre-purchased return ticket to their home country (Engelbrekt 1994: 39). In contrast to these restrictive measures, Bulgaria unilaterally lifted its visa requirements for EU and EFTA countries on 10 March 1997, a step clearly intended to inspire the reciprocal lifting of the visa requirements on Bulgarian nationals travelling to Western Europe. However, EU member states are unlikely to relax their visa policies until the country improves its border controls and implements efficient asylum procedures.[1]

THE CZECH REPUBLIC

The Czech Republic joined the international refugee regime in 1990 under the Czechoslovak Constitution. Before this date, the Czechoslovak Constitution of July 1960 provided an article relating to asylum (Art. 33), but this was more an instrument of the Communist regime than an expression of the principles and norms of the international refugee regime. After the democratic revolution in late 1989, the Ministry of the Interior initially refused to issue decisions on asylum cases until concrete guidelines were established (Warning 1991: 24). At the same time, the opening up of the country's borders allowed growing numbers of foreigners to enter in transit in order to emigrate either legally or illegally to the countries of Western Europe and Germany in particular. Nevertheless, tight controls at the German border led many of these migrants to stay in Czechoslovakia. Accordingly, the numbers of asylum seekers began to rise (Warning 1991).[2] As a consequence, the government began to establish reception centres and prepared the adoption of specific asylum regulations.

Czechoslovakia signed the Geneva Refugee Convention and its New York Protocol in November 1991, effective as of February 1992. In October 1990, a law on refugees was passed which came into force in January 1991 and provides the basic procedures for refugee status determination and the rights and duties of asylum seekers and refugees. A second relevant instrument is the law of March 1992 concerning the stay of foreigners. In 1993 amendments of Article 11 of the asylum law introduced an accelerated procedure for 'manifestly unfounded' cases, which were to include cases of asylum seekers from so-called 'safe countries of origin'.

The general framework for the adoption of these laws was established in January 1991, when the Czechoslovak Federal Assembly passed an amendment to the constitution entitled the Bill of Fundamental Rights and Liberties. The bill stated that all international agreements on human rights and basic freedoms ratified by Czechoslovakia, including those on foreigners and refugees, were binding for all Czechoslovak citizens and took precedence over other domestic laws. After the dissolution of Czechoslovakia at the end of 1992, the Czech Republic stuck to these international and domestic instruments, and the Bill of Fundamental Rights and Liberties became one of the pillars of the constitutional order of the Czech Republic.

The refugee law of 1990, as amended in 1993, provides the basis for Czech asylum policy. As a general rule, foreigners wishing to apply for refugee status must submit their application at the border. However, exceptions are made in cases of 'objective reasons'.[3] Formally, the Alien's Law stipulates that an alien can enter the Czech Republic exclusively on the basis of a valid travel document and, where necessary, a visa. However, this rule does not apply to asylum seekers, who should not be denied access to asylum procedures on these grounds (CAHAR 1997: 2). The competent authority which decides on asylum applications for refugee status in the first administrative instance is the Directorate of the Alien and Border Police Service of the Police Presidium in the Ministry of the Interior. A first appeal against a negative decision may be lodged with the Ministry of the Interior, and review is foreseen with the higher administrative court. Until June 1993, asylum seekers were in practice allowed to remain in the Czech Republic pending judicial review.

In the first years, the general refugee policy followed quite liberal and relatively unformalised guidelines. Furthermore, temporary protection was granted to persons from the former Yugoslavia who did normally not fulfil the criteria of a convention refugee on an *ad hoc* basis. In addition, the rather liberal approach towards aliens living and working on Czech territory meant that many aliens did not consider it necessary to apply for formal refugee status while staying in the country.

This line of policy has changed since 1993 when a first restrictive reform of the asylum law was adopted in December of that year.[4] The amendments are designed to shorten the duration of the asylum procedures in general,[5] and more specifically to introduce accelerated procedures for 'manifestly unfounded' cases. This notion refers to applicants who do not co-operate in the examination of their claims and who come from a state where, on the basis of generally accepted facts, there is no persecution in the sense of the Refugee Act. Furthermore, it applies to cases where the citizenship of the applicant signifies the responsibility of another state, to applicants who have committed serious crimes, and to persons applying on exclusively economic grounds. In manifestly unfounded cases, the decision should be taken within seven days and an appeal must be made within three days following that decision. With this notion, the Czech Republic has introduced the concept of 'safe country of origin' as laid down in the London Conclusions adopted by the EU Ministers of the Interior on 31 November–1 December 1992 (see Chapter 2).

In addition, new asylum legislation is being drafted which will bring the Czech Republic into line with EU standards on manifestly unfounded asylum applications, the principles of 'safe country of origin' and of 'safe third country' (EC Commission 1997a: 10). This is partly a reaction to the signing of a readmission agreement with Germany in November 1994 and partly an integral component of the country's preparation for EU membership. From a German perspective, the signing of the readmission agreement was motivated by the high numbers of illegal migrants transiting through the Czech Republic in order to enter Germany. In 1993 alone, German border guards detained some 19,000 people trying to cross into Germany illegally from the Czech Republic. The number of those who did manage to cross undetected is unknown. At the same time, the Czech police detained about 24,000 illegal immigrants (Pehe 1994: 32). One way used by Germany to curb this immigration was the reform of its asylum legislation in July 1993 introducing the principles of the 'safe country of origin' and the 'safe third country'. Another related measure was the negotiation of readmission agreements in order to efficiently reject illegal immigrants and asylum seekers on 'safe third country' grounds at the border. The negotiations with the Czech Republic took time, since the two countries disagreed on the length of time during which the German authorities would be able to return illegal immigrants. Furthermore, the Czech Republic apparently tried to delay concluding such a treaty with Germany until it had signed readmission agreements with its own Eastern neighbours and other major emigrant-producing countries. Failure to do so would have left the Czech Republic unable to deport illegal immigrants expelled from Germany. Hence, readmission agreements were concluded with the Slovak Republic (valid as of 1 January 1993), Austria (1 November 1992), Poland (30 October 1993), and Romania (26 May 1994), before the agreement with Germany was signed on 23 November 1994 (valid as of 1 January 1995). On 5 August 1995, an agreement with Hungary came into force. Other agreements are being prepared with Canada, Slovenia, Ukraine, Belarus, Russia, France and the Netherlands (EP 1997: 29).

Apart from the signing of readmission agreements, joining the international refugee regime and the subsequent adaptation to Western European policies was accompanied by measures to strengthen border controls, the fight against illegal immigration including trafficking in human beings, and the imposition of restrictive visa requirements on persons originating from emigration-producing countries. This has had a significant impact on

Czech foreign policy. Given its geographical position and its historical ties, visa-free agreements were concluded with the former countries of the Soviet Union and the Balkan states. In order to prevent immigration, however, the Czech authorities require persons from these countries to present a formal invitation and to have sufficient means for the time of stay in the country.

The key foreign policy dimension of these processes is most salient in the case of the Czech-Slovak relations. Originally, after the separation of Czechoslovakia, the two countries had agreed to keep their common borders open, allowing the free movement of persons. This situation changed in spring 1993 when Germany, in the final stage of the reform of its asylum law, pressed the Czech government to establish a regular border with the Slovak Republic in order to avoid uncontrolled migration to its territory. By way of response, the acting Prime Minister of Slovakia, Vladimir Meciar, accused the Czechs and Germans of trying to build a new 'iron curtain' between the East and the West (Fisher 1994: 43). This conflict was finally resolved with an agreement between the Czech and Slovak Republics that their citizens would not be subject to the new border controls, but the German initiative had nevertheless put an unexpected strain on the relations between the two countries.

HUNGARY

Hungary was the first Eastern bloc country to join the international refugee regime while still under a Communist government in 1989. This move was not so much an expression of its liberal commitment to international protection as a means of admitting large numbers of ethnic Hungarians wishing to re-enter the country. The Hungarian Constitution of 1949 contained an asylum provision, but as this right could only be exercised by the government, it did not amount to a participation in the international refugee regime.[6] Until the mid-1980s, the Hungarian government had made little use of this instrument of political discretion,[7] but the situation changed dramatically at the end of 1987, when large numbers of ethnic Hungarians from Transylvania fled to Hungary from discrimination under the Romanian dictator, Nicolae Ceausescu. It is assumed that during the mid-1980s, close to two million ethnic Hungarians lived in Romania (Fullerton 1996: 506). By the end of 1988, there were more than 13,000 refugees in Hungary, of which 95 per cent were ethnic Hungarians from Romania (Fullerton 1996: 506). This influx continued to rise in 1989 and, despite the overthrow of Ceaucescu in December 1989, reached a peak in 1990 with a total of over 18,000 asylum seekers coming to Hungary, of which 15,000 were ethnic Hungarians (Fullerton 1996: 507). Initially, these persons did not undergo any formal asylum procedures; they were implicitly recognised by the Hungarian government and admitted with great tolerance (Pataki 1994: 34).

The second important group of refugees entering Hungary came from the former German Democratic Republic. In late 1989, some 10,000 East Germans fled to Hungary and prompted the government to open the border to Austria, thereby allowing them to reach the Federal Republic of Germany.

While the East German refugees entered Hungary only in transit, the country faced a new wave of immigration with the outbreak of civil war in the former Yugoslavia. Given Hungary's geographical proximity, large numbers of Croats, Bosnians and later ethnic Hungarians from the Vojvodina, sought shelter on its territory. According to the Hungarian Office of Refugees and Migration Affairs, the country received a total of 133,000 refugees between 1988 and 1995. Of these, 54,000 were from Romania and 76,000 from ex-Yugoslavia.[8]

Hungary's decision to join the international refugee regime was a reaction to the continued influx of ethnic Hungarian refugees from Transylvania. The adoption of an asylum law was seen as a means of repatriating these persons in their 'home' country. In March 1989, the Communist government of Hungary was the first Eastern-bloc country to sign the Geneva Convention and its New

York Protocol. However, it put a ceiling on its international obligations by stipulating that it would not accept refugees from outside Europe. In the same year, the constitutional asylum provision was reformed as part of a major revision of the national constitution. In contrast to the earlier regulation, this reform implemented the international refugee definition of the Geneva Convention.[9] Although this article does not mention the geographical limitation, it originally did not apply to non-European refugees, and remained in force until 1998 despite repeated promises to lift the limitation. Until the removal of this limitation, two different asylum procedures existed in practice: one governed by national legislation for refugees of European origins, and one regulated by the UNHCR for non-Europeans on the basis of an informal agreement with the Hungarian government. In practice, if the UNHCR considered an applicant to meet the conditions for refugee status, the Hungarian government usually issued a temporary residence permit. The argument given for the preservation of the geographical limitation was the fear of being overburdened by refugees from all over the world who could not be integrated into Hungarian society (Pataki 1994: 35; Fullerton 1996). With the new law, Hungary has also adapted its regulations to the EU 'acquis' and has introduced the concept of the 'safe third country' together with simplified procedures in asylum cases which are 'manifestly unfounded'.

The actual national asylum procedure for European refugees is based on the Refugee Act CXXXIX of 1998 amending the governmental decree on the refugee recognition procedure passed in October 1989 implementing the provisions of the Geneva Convention and its Protocol.[10] The competent authority for European asylum seekers is the local unit of the Department of Refugee Affairs of the Ministry of the Interior. The request for asylum should be made within seventy-two hours of crossing the frontier with the police, a border guard or reception centre for refugees. Appeal against a negative decision can be made in the first instance to the Department of Refugee Affairs of the Ministry of the Interior. If this decision is negative, the applicant may appeal to the courts.

With the 1998 reform, Hungary has introduced accelerated procedures in cases of 'safe country of origin' and has adopted the 'safe third country' rule. Accordingly, asylum seekers are denied access to asylum procedures if they have stayed or transited in a safe third country before lodging their claim in Hungary. With this reform, Hungary has–de jure–brought its asylum law into line with EU requirements.

In recent years, several provisions of the asylum practice have been criticised by the UNHCR (UNHCR 1995d), other humanitarian agencies and the European Parliament (EP 1997: 40). Apart from the fact that the geographical limitation constituted a severe restriction of the Geneva Convention, the seventy-two hour deadline for applications carried the risk that an application would be refused merely on procedural grounds. Another point of concern was the amount of unwritten, informal administrative practices which govern the actual asylum procedure. In particular, the application of informal pre-screening practices by the Hungarian authorities has met with strong criticism. These practices not only included the concept of 'safe third countries' without any formal legal basis (EC Commission 1997a: 16), but were also used by the border police to favour the entry of refugees of Hungarian descent who, until 1998, made up 80 per cent of the applicants allowed to instigate the procedure of first instance (EP 1997: 40).[11] Furthermore, recent reforms have authorised the security police, normally responsible for investigating criminal cases, to deal with refugees arriving at Budapest airport (EP 1997). Finally, the European Commission has observed that although Hungary is party to the European Convention of Human Rights and Fundamental Freedoms, there are no formal procedural guarantees or other national legislation to ensure its implementation (EC Commission 1997a: 16).

In retrospect, the most striking characteristic of Hungarian refugee policy so far has been the divergence between the high numbers of persons seeking refuge in the country and the very limited number of persons formally recognised under the asylum procedure. Out of the total of 133,000 refugees entering the country between 1988 and 1995, only 5,000 filed asylum claims and followed the recognition process through to the end. Of these, roughly 4,000 received formal refugee status, most of whom were ethnic Hungarians (Fullerton 1996: 521; EP 1997: 37).

Hence, it follows that under the old regulation, the bulk of persons seeking refuge in Hungary did not start formal asylum procedures. In the case of refugees from the former Yugoslavia, temporary protection was offered on an informal and humanitarian basis for a limited period of time. However, when Austria closed its borders to refugees from Bosnia and Herzegovina in summer 1992, Hungary, apprehensive of being overwhelmed by refugees, also started to restrict its policies (Pataki 1994: 36). These restrictions, which were applied informally at the outset, became legally valid under the 1998 reform.

Like the other associated countries of Central and Eastern Europe, the Hungarian government has accompanied its refugee policy with a wide range of measures to counter illegal immigration. Since 1989 border control has changed significantly in order to meet Western European standards. In 1991, stricter rules were introduced to ensure a consistent check on the requirements for entry into the country, such as the validity of travel documents, visas, money required to stay in Hungary and so forth. Between 1993 and 1995, almost 1.5 million people were refused entry at the border (EP 1997: 36). In 1992, the head of the Hungarian border police complained that Hungary had become the 'waiting room of Western Europe' for irregular migrants (*Migration News Sheet,* June 1992). In the same year, the Hungarian Border Guard was reorganised in order to reduce illegal migration and trafficking in human beings, for example through the replacement of enlisted personnel with professional staff or the creation of special organisations such as the Directorates' Investigations Group and the Action Service of the Border Guard. Finally, in 1994 a new act to regulate the entry of aliens was passed and reinforces the powers of the Hungarian authorities to restrict entry at their borders. Technological innovations were introduced which will prepare the country for accession to the Schengen Agreement. In line with these developments, Hungary concluded readmission agreements with several countries in order to facilitate the return of undesired aliens.[12] Another area where Hungary has adapted to the EU 'acquis' is its visa policy. With the opening of membership talks with the EU in April 1998, Hungary announced the introduction of transit visas for passengers coming from certain countries changing flights at Hungarian airports in order to curb illegal immigration. At the same time, it announced that border controls would be significantly strengthened. Despite these efforts to comply with EU requirements, Hungary has strongly opposed pressure, in particular from Austria, to impose visa requirements on Romanians, which would significantly affect its relationship with the Hungarian minority living in Romania. Caught between the requirements of EU membership and its interests *vis-à-vis* ethnic minorities, Hungary is considering the adoption of alternative solutions such as multiple-entry visas valid for ten years for the Hungarian minorities in Romania, Slovakia, Yugoslavia and Ukraine (*Migration News Sheet*, July 1998).

POLAND

Poland, in common with most Central and Eastern European countries, only joined the international refugee regime after the collapse of Communism in the early 1990s. Article 88 of the 1952 constitution provided a formal right to asylum, which, as in the other CEECs, was more a strategic instrument of the government than a recognition of international human rights norms. With the ratification of the Geneva Convention and its 1967 Protocol in September 1991, this article was adjusted to the Geneva Convention and now reads 'Nationals of other states and stateless persons may enjoy the right of asylum as stipulated in the law'.

Poland's accession to the international refugee regime was clearly induced by its early incorporation into Western European policies with the signature of the readmission agreement with the

Schengen countries in 1991. Until the 1990s, Poland did not have large numbers of immigrants or refugees. The situation started to change in summer 1990, when roughly 600 asylum seekers were returned to Poland after they had attempted to cross the Swedish border (Steiner and Sladewski 1995: 233). It is estimated that between November 1989 and early 1990, some 7,000 asylum seekers had taken this route to Sweden, and in March 1990, the Swedish authorities closed the borders following bilateral discussions with the Polish government (Stainsby 1990: 636). Poland's transformation from a transit to a receiving country for asylum seekers and voluntary migrants heading towards Western Europe was supported by the conclusion of the readmission agreement with the Schengen countries. This agreement provides for the responsibility to take back not only own-state nationals who stay in a Schengen state illegally, but also other third-state nationals, including asylum-seekers.

Unlike the early ratification of the Geneva Convention, Poland has not yet passed specific legal provisions regulating the asylum procedure. A new Aliens Act which regulates the entry into, transit through, sojourn in, and departure from the territory for aliens is, however, expected to be adopted soon, which will include provisions on refugees and asylum seekers. Until that time, the asylum procedure is governed by the Aliens Act of 1963 as amended in 1991 and a mixture of general administrative procedural law and informal practices.

Persons seeking refuge in Poland can either apply to the Polish Border Guard at the border or, once inside the country, directly to the Minister of Interior at the Office for Migration and Refugee Affairs. This office, created in February 1993, is the competent authority for decisions on asylum claims, taken after consultation with the Minister of Foreign Affairs. A first appeal against this decision can be lodged again at the Ministry of the Interior, and a second judicial review can be sought with the Supreme Administrative Court. Apart from formal refugee status, the Polish legislation contains no provisions regarding temporary protection.

Under the present asylum procedure, Poland does not formally apply pre-screening measures such as the 'safe third country' rule, the 'safe country of origin', or the concept of 'manifestly unfounded asylum claims'. However, these notions will be introduced with the new Aliens Act. According to the Polish government, the draft act will 'prevent the abuse of asylum procedures' and is 'in accordance with the general trend in implementing stricter asylum policy in the EU member states.'[13] Article 35.3 of the new Act excludes the initiation of an asylum procedure in 'safe country' cases and for manifestly unfounded asylum claims.

On the one hand, the restrictive reform of the domestic laws is a preparation for EU membership, and on the other it is supported by the increasing numbers of refugees seeking asylum in Poland due to the implementation of readmission agreements with Western states and the strengthening of border controls. Until recently, Poland was predominantly a transit country for foreigners travelling to Western Europe. Since 1994, however, the number of asylum applications in Poland has increased considerably (EP 1997: 52). This increase is partly attributable to the number of asylum seekers sent back by Germany on the basis of the readmission agreement concluded in 1993. In 1995, 9,098 persons were returned to Poland from Western countries, of which 8,630 came from Germany in accordance with the readmission agreement, and a total of 4,064 third-country nationals, of whom 492 were asylum seekers who had crossed the common German-Polish border illegally (Danish Refugee Council 1998). Given that Poland constitutes the most important transit country for illegal immigrants and asylum seekers on their way to Germany, this agreement, together with the readmission agreement between Poland and the Schengen states, plays a central role in Germany's new asylum policy and its attempt to limit the intake of asylum seekers. Apart from the obligation to readmit own-state and other third-country nationals who have passed through Poland on their way to Germany, the agreement provides for a range of co-operation measures to help fight illegal immigration, to strengthen borders and to establish asylum procedures. As a compensation for Poland's willingness to co-operate, this agreement has been accompanied by a financial transfer of 150 million DM, of which 49 per cent is officially allocated to border security, 38 per cent to the police, but only 13 per cent for the establishment of an asylum infrastructure (*Bundestagsdrucksache* 13/6030, 30 October 1996). In order to be able to return unwanted aliens, the Polish authorities have signed other readmission agreements with Bulgaria, Greece, Croatia, the Czech Republic, Hungary, Moldovia, Slovakia, Romania and Ukraine. Readmission provisions are also included in the agreements on visa-free traffic with Austria, Estonia, Latvia, Lithuania, and Switzerland. Finally, readmission agreements have been negotiated with Belarus, Russia, Sweden, Canada, China and India (EP 1997: 51). The application of such a readmission agreement with Belarus, Ukraine or Russia to asylum seekers on the grounds of the 'safe third country' rule would constitute a violation of the basic norms of refugee law, in particular that of non-refoulement, since these countries do not provide refugee status determination procedures (Danish Refugee Council 1998).

The conclusion of readmission agreements has been accompanied by a general enforcement of border control, and a stepping up of police activity and communication technology. Apart from the financial resources allocated by Germany, Poland has received 15.4 million ECU in the framework of the PHARE programme for a further tightening of the eastern border and the development of a more efficient information and communication system (EP 1997: 51). According to information from the European Parliament, 18,000 persons have been readmitted in the framework of the readmission agreement with Germany from the date of its conclusion in May 1993 until end of 1996 (EP 1997: 52). At the same time, the number of migrants prevented from crossing the Polish-German border has grown significantly (Weydenthal 1994: 39).[14] These developments are complemented by measures to facilitate the effective expulsion of illegal aliens. The Polish government regards these processes as an adaptation to EU legislation and practice, which is part of the national strategy for integration (Polish government 1997: 56). Part of this strategy is also the approximation of its visa policy, which, in common with other CEECs, has created friction with the affected countries and with sections of the Polish population. In particular, the tightening up of entry procedures for visitors from Belarus and Russia, who were requested to show authenticated vouchers proving payment of accommodation or genuine invitations from Polish citizens, sparked off a wave of protest. Such measures were seen as seriously damaging cross-border trade with these countries as well as the employment of migrants in the construction industry and agriculture (*Süddeutsche Zeitung,* 28 January 1998). Nevertheless, with the onset of accession talks with the EU in April 1998, Poland was again urged to tighten its visa regimes *vis-à-vis* its eastern neighbours.

ROMANIA

Romania is generally seen as a major country of emigration. In the last years of Nicolae Ceausescu's dictatorship, large numbers of Romanians sought asylum in Western countries, and this wave of emigration was intensified after the overthrow of the Communist regime (Shafir 1994: 41). Yet since 1991 Romania itself has been increasingly receiving refugees from Africa, the Far East and the Middle East.

Romania's accession to the Geneva Convention and its New York Protocol in summer 1991 was clearly induced by its increasing involvement in bilateral and multilateral activities with EU member states. In the same year, Article 18 of the Romanian Constitution was adopted and stipulates that 'asylum status is granted and withdrawn according to the provisions of the law, observing the international treaties and conventions signed by Romania' (quoted in EC commission 1997a: 24). Despite the declarations, asylum decisions were mostly taken on an *ad hoc* basis. An inter-ministerial body, the Romanian Committee for Migration, was set up in June 1991 and is responsible for making decisions on asylum requests and other immigrant matters (Shafir 1994: 42). A genuine asylum law took five years to come into force with the Law concerning the Status and the Regime of Refugees in Romania of April 1996. The new law distinguishes between three categories of refugees, 'Convention' (Art. 1), 'humanitarian' (Art. 2), and 'war' refugees (Art. 5). The competence to decide on asylum applications has been transferred to a commission composed of representatives from the Ministries of the Interior, Foreign Affairs, and Labour and Social Protection appointed by the government. While this committee is responsible for the recognition of refugee status, the actual examination of an asylum claim is made by a different agency, the newly created Refugee Office of the General Directorate of Border Police, Aliens, Migration Problems and Passports of the Ministry of the Interior. This division of competences has been repeatedly criticised, since the commission does not have specialised personnel with the necessary knowledge in asylum matters (EC Commission 1997a: 24; UNHCR 1997). Appeal against a negative decision can be lodged with a court of first instance.

Although not mentioned explicitly in the law, the Romanian authorities implicitly apply the notion of the 'safe third country', in so far as Article 6 of the law provides that asylum seekers without document or visa 'will be authorised to enter Romania [...] if he has arrived directly from the territory where his life or liberty is threatened.' (quoted in EC Commission 1997a: 24). Thus, applicants who have travelled through a safe third country will be denied entry by the border guards. According to a government decision relating to the implementation of the law, this also included countries which have not signed the Geneva Convention (Danish Refugee Council 1998). In much the same way as Bulgaria, the 'safe third country' notion is applied without proper consideration of the actual human rights situation or the implementation of the Geneva Convention in the country concerned. Considering that the Romanian asylum law does not contain any reference to the universal principles of the Geneva Convention and that it only stipulates the principle of non-refoulement for recognised refugees, this application of the 'safe third country' rule is likely to lead to direct or indirect refoulement of persons in need of protection (UNHCR 1997: 4). This tendency is reinforced by the fact that such pre-screening measures confer authority on the border guards or the police, who are not necessarily trained in refugee matters. Furthermore, the Romanian asylum law has been criticised for excluding asylum seekers from refugee status on the basis of criminal activity or failure to meet a time limit for submitting an asylum application which 'could in principle be used to exclude from refugee status any asylum seeker who has breached *any* of Romania's laws.' (Danish Refugee Council 1998). Finally, the Romanian asylum law is further criticised for a provision in its Article 22 which limits the duration of refugee status to three years, with the option of an extension for a maximum of another two years (UNHCR 1997: 3; EP 1997: 58).

At the same time as entering the international refugee regime, Romania has begun to curb illegal immigration. Since 1993, the Romanian authorities have tightened border controls in order to identify false documents and to combat trafficking in human beings. PHARE money has been used to modernise border posts, and border police officials have received additional training. In addition to these domestic measures, readmission agreements have been concluded with Austria, the Benelux countries, the Czech Republic, France, Germany, Greece, Hungary, India, Italy, Poland, Slovakia, Slovenia, Spain, Sweden and Switzerland since 1990 (EP 1997: 56). Finally, Romania has also imposed restrictive visa requirements on the main refugee producing countries and requires visitors from these countries to bring sufficient funding for their stay as well as a pre-purchased return ticket (Shafir 1994: 45). Romanian citizens, like their Bulgarian neighbours, still require visas to enter Western Europe.

SLOVENIA

The Republic of Slovenia acceded to the Geneva Convention and its New York Protocol in July 1992 by succession from the former Yugoslavia. As of 1991, the country has hosted large numbers of temporarily displaced persons fleeing civil war in the other parts of the former Yugoslavia. Due its special exposure to this group of refugees, Slovenia has concentrated on the issue of temporary protection for civil war refugees. Accordingly, while a comprehensive law on asylum is still in preparation, a law on temporary refuge came into force on 25 April 1997.

At the constitutional level, the right to asylum is guaranteed to persons subject to 'persecution for their stand on human rights and fundamental freedoms' (Art. 48 of the Slovenian Constitution, quoted in UNHCR 1992: 2). Until the new law comes into force, Slovenia's asylum procedure is governed by the 1991 Law on Foreigners. This law contains several articles which deal with refugee determination procedures and the rights of recognised refugees. According to the law, asylum seekers must apply for asylum within three days of their arrival in the country. In practice, a first screening of asylum applications is made by the police, who conduct a short interview to determine the admissibility of the claim. Here, an indirect use of the 'safe third country' rule is made. Due to the lack of legislation and guidelines, it is feared that guarantees regarding readmission, access to procedures for determining status against further refoulement and subjection to inhuman or degrading treatment are not systematically examined before returns are made (Danish Refugee Council 1998). If accepted, the claim is examined by the Asylum Section of the Department for Foreigners at the Ministry of the Interior, which is the authority competent to grant refugee status. If the decision is negative, an appeal can be lodged with the government of the Republic of Slovenia and in second instance with the Supreme Court. The draft asylum law aims at a full harmonisation with the 'acquis' established by the member states of the European Union and will include safe country notions.

In sum, it must be said that the asylum system is only now beginning to take shape. To date, apart from temporary protection, few refugees have lodged an asylum request in Slovenia.[15] Nevertheless, this country has made some efforts to combat illegal immigration and to strengthen its border controls. Readmission agreements have been signed with Austria, Hungary, Croatia, Italy, Poland, Greece, Romania, Canada, France, the Benelux countries, Slovakia, Switzerland and Lithuania, and agreements with Poland, Bulgaria, Bosnia, Macedonia, the Czech Republic, Denmark, Estonia and Latvia are being prepared (EP 1997: 64). In order to fight illegal migration the Slovenian police has developed close co-operative ties with neighbouring countries and the main destination countries, for example Germany. This co-operation includes information exchange and the co-ordination of measures for the prevention and investigation of trafficking in human beings and the detection of forged documents.

SLOVAKIA

The first years of the Slovak refugee policy and their experience under the Czechoslovakian Constitution mirror the Czech experience. The first generation of legislation on foreigners and refugees was adopted by the Czechoslovak parliament after the fall of Communism in 1989. Slovakia acceded to the international treaties signed by Czechoslovakia after it separated from the Czech Republic in January 1993. Until 1995, the Slovak asylum system was to a large extent governed by the legislation passed by Czechoslovakia in the early 1990s. According to Chapter 53 of the Constitution, the Slovak Republic grants asylum to foreigners who are persecuted for exercising their political rights and freedoms (quoted in EC Commission 1997a: 26). A new asylum law was adopted in late 1995, effective as of January 1996, which is designed to harmonise national refugee policy with that of the EU member states and determines that the state agency competent for dealing with refugee issues in the first instance is the Migration Office of the Ministry of the Interior. Persons failing to apply for asylum within twenty-four hours of entering the country may be denied access on procedural grounds (Art. 4). If the decision taken by the Migration Office is negative, an appeal can be lodged with the Minister of the Interior and with the Supreme Court in the second instance. In accordance to the 'acquis' of the EU member states, the new asylum law includes the notions of 'safe third country' and 'safe country of origin'. The arrival of an applicant in Slovakia from one of these countries does not constitute a *de jure* obstacle, and such claims are examined in accelerated procedures (CAHAR 1997: 25; Hoskova 1996: 131). Nevertheless, one can safely assume that in many instances asylum seekers are denied access to asylum procedures at the border (Danish Refugee Council 1998). One particularly negative characteristic of the law is that its definition of a 'safe country' makes no reference to the Geneva Convention or the European Convention of Human Rights and Fundamental Freedoms, the only stated criteria being the existence of a constitutional and democratic order.[16] Another criticism raised by the UNHCR is that, given the very short time limit of twenty-four hours for the submission of asylum applications, refugees may be denied access to the procedure and simply refouled to the country from which they have come (EP 1997: 61).

In addition to these restrictions in asylum regulation, Slovakia has tried to enhance its ability to limit illegal immigration. In 1994, a law was passed which restricts entry into Slovakia. It stipulates visa requirements on citizens of several former Soviet republics and some parts of ex-Yugoslavia, imposed after the Czech Republic, Hungary and Poland had enacted similar restrictions (Fisher 1994: 42–43). In addition, border controls have been tightened and readmission agreements were concluded with all neighbouring countries (Austria, Hungary, Ukraine, Poland, Czech Republic) and with Romania, Bulgaria, Croatia and Slovenia.

THE BALTIC STATES

The three Baltic states,[17] Estonia, Latvia and Lithuania, were the last associated CEECs to join the international refugee regime in 1997. The lateness of their accession was caused by the fear of the potential financial burden resulting from the obligations of refugee protection. Given their geographical location and the previously non-existent borders with Russia, these countries feared becoming overburdened with refugees and asylum seekers coming from and through Russia and whose continuation for Western Europe they would be obliged to prevent.

In July 1995, the Lithuanian Parliament adopted a Law on the Status of Refugees drafted with the aid of Scandinavian experts and including the 'safe third country' concept which has not yet been fully implemented. In addition, the administrative infrastructure for the examination of asylum claims is currently being established (EC Commission 1997a: 20; CAHAR 1997: 8). Before its adoption, Lithuania concluded readmission agreements with the two other Baltic states, and with Bulgaria, Cyprus, Malta, Poland, Slovenia, Switzerland and its Scandinavian neighbours, Norway and Finland (EP 1997: 47; Intergovernmental Consultations 1997).

In Estonia, a Law on Refugees was adopted in February 1997. It regulates the admission, legal status and the grounds for residence in Estonia for asylum seekers and refugees, and contains the 'safe third country' notion. Like Lithuania, Estonia signed readmission agreements with most neighbouring countries (Latvia, Lithuania, Finland and Denmark).

The third Baltic state, Latvia, was the last one to accede to the Geneva Convention in June 1997. According to the information from the European Parliament, Latvia's authorities gave three reasons for their initial opposition to join the international refugee regime. Firstly, most persons entering Latvia do not want to apply for asylum there but to continue to another country. Secondly, Latvia fears becoming a host country for persons whose asylum requests have been rejected in EU member states. Finally, the Latvian government argues that considering the country's geographical position, it would only join the international refugee regime on the grounds that it can in turn ensure the return of illegal immigrants and rejected asylum seekers. This would require the conclusion of readmission accords with Russia and Belarus (EP 1997: 45). As the last states in the chain of return agreements, all three Baltic states are eager to conclude such agreements with their eastern neighbours in order to pass on this new Western European instrument of immigration control.

The decision to finally sign the Geneva Convention must thus be seen as a strategic move in Latvia's attempts to become a member of the European Union. Latvia's reluctance is, however, illustrated by the fact that the Convention was originally only adopted for European refugees, thus applying the geographical limitation—only removed in 1998 due to pressure from Western countries. As with other CEECs, one of the means applied by, among others, Finland and Sweden to push Latvia to join the international refugee regime was the maintenance of visa requirements for Latvian citizens until the geographical limitation was lifted (*Migration News Sheet,* September 1997). Similar strategies were successfully applied to make the Latvian government reconsider its citizenship policy towards the large Russian minority in Latvia.

As in the other CEECs, the Baltic countries' adaptation to the EU asylum 'acquis' is only one focal point in an extensive transformation process which concentrates on the re-organisation of border regimes in these countries. In accordance with Western concerns to limit 'unwanted' migration, this transformation implied the redefinition of the borders of the Baltic states with Russia and Belarus and the erection of stringent border regimes. While until a few years ago, no controls were imposed on the movement of persons between the Baltic states and their Central and Eastern European neighbours, these countries are now very active in the closure of their borders and in the prevention of illegal immigrants in transit to the West. In a recent analysis, these processes were seen as turning the Baltic countries into 'Europe's new doorkeepers' for asylum seekers and voluntary migrants heading West (Leuthardt 1997).

CONCLUSION

The survey of recent changes in the asylum legislation of the countries of Central and Eastern Europe shows a clear trend: despite internal socio-economic difficulties in most of them, all ten associated countries have made considerable efforts to join the international refugee regime and to strengthen their borders against illegal entry and transit. While the situation varies greatly across the CEECs, the speed of the legislative and administrative innovations suggests that they will increasingly be considered 'safe' by their Western neighbours—thereby allowing increasing numbers of asylum seekers to be sent back to these countries.

One must not lose sight of the fact that the CEEC's participation in refugee protection is not only a result of a shift towards liberal values nor an expression of a humanitarian commitment, but is also a concession to Western European concerns to limit their own exposure to flows of asylum seekers, refugees and voluntary migrants. Central and Eastern Europe's accession to the European refugee regime is an asymmetrical process in which Western European interests prevail. It was induced by the policies of single Western European countries at a unilateral or bilateral level which effectively incorporated the CEECs into the emerging EU refugee regime. The main instruments in this process were the tightening of border controls and entry conditions, the introduction of the 'safe country' rules, and the conclusion of readmission agreements to facilitate the expulsion of illegal immigrants and the rejection of asylum seekers. With this set of policies, the EU countries effectively transferred their intra-communitarian system of negative redistribution for handling asylum claims to the neighbouring countries of Central and Eastern Europe. As a result of these measures, the CEECs are rapidly being transformed from former emigration and transit countries into receiving countries. With the introduction of asylum and immigration matters on the requirements for EU membership, the CEECs' adaptation to the EU 'acquis' has gained its final political legitimation.

This involvement of Central and Eastern Europe in an emerging pan-European refugee regime, however, is problematic in several respects. Firstly, the CEECs have not participated in formulating the policies which now affect them and which they are now compelled to adopt if they wish to join the Union. Secondly, the incorporation of these states into Western European asylum policies occurred prior to their adoption of the basic legal and institutional infrastructure for the protection of refugees. As a result, their adaptation to the EU 'acquis' requires far more than the mere adoption of EU regulations. Rather, it presupposes a set of institutional transformations ranging from, for example, border regimes, the judicial system and administration, to the implementation of international humanitarian norms. In Western Europe, these pillars of liberal regimes have evolved slowly over several decades, whereas in Eastern Europe the CEECs are under pressure to adopt them as swiftly as possible. This shift towards liberal values and institutions, required for the asylum system to meet international standards, is impeded not only by this sense of urgency but also by the fact that the extension of the EU refugee regime is inspired more by security considerations than by humanitarian concerns. Western European endeavours to include the CEECs in their system of co-operation are induced by their concern about large-scale immigration to their territories both from and through Central and Eastern Europe. Until the mid-1990s, Western states' activities in relation to the CEECs focused almost exclusively on the fight against illegal immigration and the strengthening of Eastern borders. And even if Western policy-makers have now recognised the need to implement equitable asylum systems in these countries, the sealing of Eastern borders and the fight against illegal immigration continue to be their first priority. This is reflected not only in the bilateral co-operation programmes, but also in the priorities set by the European

Commission in the pre-accession strategies in justice and home affairs, which focus on the development of tight border management systems in all the CEECs.[18]

The perception of potential floods of refugees fleeing civil war, political instability and economic scarcity was constructed as a new threat to Western states' internal security, that is, their social stability and economic well-being. Accordingly, both bilateral activities such as co-operation programmes or financial aid and multilateral conferences have been dominated by the aim of preventing migrants reaching Western Europe. It was only after the introduction of restrictive policies such as the 'safe third country' rule or the conclusion of readmission agreements that the West recognised the fundamental need to establish some sort of asylum procedures in the CEECs and to assure their compliance with basic standards of international human rights. Hence, EU member states started to support the ratification of international agreements such as the Geneva Refugee Convention and its New York Protocol or the European Convention on Human Rights and Fundamental Freedoms. In addition, the domestic implementation of asylum legislation and refugee determination procedures was promoted through the organisation of international conferences, seminars and direct exchange programmes between member-state officials and the competent authorities of the associated countries. Here too, the shift towards the humanitarian contents of refugee policy was not only inspired by normative considerations but also by the sheer necessity of making the system of negative redistribution established with the 'safe third country' rule and the readmission agreements function effectively. Indeed, both the definition of a country as 'safe' and the application of readmission agreements presuppose the respective country's adherence to the human rights treaties mentioned above and the existence of basic asylum legislation and practices. In the case of Germany, the need for these human rights standards in the application of the 'safe third country' rule was made very explicit by the Constitutional Court in its ruling on the asylum reforms of 1993, where it made the constitutionality of this rule conditional on the 'establishment of certainty' ('*normative*

Vergewisserung) about the actual observation of these basic human rights standards when establishing the 'safety' of a third country.

Considering this dominance of Western European interests, Central and Eastern Europe's consent to participate in this emerging pan-European refugee regime in which they function as gatekeepers for refugees and illegal immigrants heading towards Western Europe must be seen as the result of a political bargain in exchange for the prospect of EU membership. As the declarations made by representatives of the associated countries show, the CEECs are very conscious of the potential burden incurred by a stringent application of the 'safe third country' rule or readmission agreements. Their efforts to help the West control and prevent immigration and asylum flows must thus be seen as a leverage for financial support, visa-free travel for their citizens and the prospect of Union membership.[19]

Despite these efforts to meet Western requirements, the fields of asylum and immigration may still constitute major obstacles to EU enlargement. This is due, on the one hand, to the highly sensitive nature of these issues in contemporary Western societies and the high priority given to these areas by member-state governments. On the other hand, the difficulty of impeding illegal immigration and sealing territorial borders and simultaneously respecting basic humanitarian standards is a particularly formidable task for the CEECs.

In the face of this contradictory logic of co-operation in asylum and immigration matters between liberalism and restrictionism, these issues may be invoked in order to hinder early enlargement and to delay the opening up of Western job markets to the citizens of candidate countries. This is already reflected in the calls for the adoption of longer-term transition periods on the free movement of CEEC workers, proposed under the Austrian Presidency of the EU in summer 1998. Furthermore, the Schengen states made it clear at their meeting with the CEEC Ministers of the Interior that they would not allow enlargement to take place until the CEECs tightened up their borders in the sense of the Schengen 'acquis'.[20] Moreover, the European Commission appears to take a critical stance on justice and home affairs. In an interview, the Justice Commissioner, Anita Gradin, suggested that the CEECs may be hindered in their bids to join the EU unless they can seal their borders more effectively against illegal immigration and crime. Seen in this light, the enlargement process threatens to be caught in a double trap. The sealing of eastern borders may be judged as either too lax because illegal immigration still takes place, or too harsh where it does not respect the basic humanitarian and liberal values championed by the West.

NOTES

1. This is what the Bulgarian Prime Minister, Ivan Kostov, was told during his visit to Germany (*Migration New Sheet,* May 1998).

2. Here and in what follows, I have not cited empirical data because of the scarcity and inconsistency of available statistics on asylum applications, legal and illegal entries, and recognition rates.

3. Refugee Act, para. 20.

4. Act 317/1993 of 8 December 1993 amending and supplementing Act 498/1990 Concerning Refugees, effective as of 1 January 1994.

5. In particular, s. 5, para. 4 and s. 16, para. 4 of the amended law.

6. Article 67 of the 1949 Hungarian Constitution read that, 'Everyone who is persecuted for his democratic behaviour, or for his activity to enhance social progress, the liberation of peoples or the protection of peace, may be granted asylum', quoted in Fullerton (1996: 500).

7. The most important cases of refugees in Hungary at that time were some 3,000 Greek Communists fleeing the aftermath of the Greek civil war in 1940, roughly 1,000 Chilean Communists accepted in the 1970s and sporadic instances of individual revolutionaries from Africa and Asia (Fullerton 1996: 505).

8. Quoted in Fullerton (1996: note 66).

9. A variation from the definition of a refugee in Art. 1A, Geneva Convention is the recognition of persecution for linguistic reasons, see Art. 65, para. 1, Hungarian Constitution.

10. Decree 101 of 28 September 1989 on the Recognition Process of Refugees.

11. Fullerton (1996), argues that in practice, the Hungarian asylum system amounts more to a 'law of return' for ethnic Hungarians since it discriminates against non-Hungarian asylum seekers and favours ethnic Hungarians from the

moment of the application to the recognition and the granting of Hungarian citizenship.

12. Such agreements were signed with Romania, Austria, Croatia, Slovenia, Ukraine, Switzerland, Slovakia, the Czech Republic, France, Poland and Bosnia-Herzegovina (EP 1997: 37; statistics of the Intergovernmental Consultations of 17 July 1997).

13. It is important to note that in this document, which exposes the national strategy for EU integration, the part on the new asylum law is put together with visa and police co-operation in the chapter on the 'Protection of the EU external borders' (Polish government (1997: 56–57).

14. While controls at the German-Polish border are becoming more effective, illegal movements shift to the Czech borders (Czaplinski 1994: note 23).

15. According to the Slovenian Ministry of the Interior, the number of asylum applications from June 1991 until 1997 has been around 100 (EP 1997: 64).

16. Accordingly, the list of 'safe countries of origin' includes some which may well be refugee producing, such as, for example, Angola, Ghana, Kenya and Senegal (Hoskova 1996: 131).

17. The three Baltic states, Estonia, Latvia and Lithuania, are dealt with together since little can be said on their refugee policy given their very recent accession to the international refugee regime.

18. The short-term and medium-term priorities of the pre-accession strategies in the various fields of the EU 'acquis' are printed in *Uniting Europe* No. 2, 13 April 1998; No. 3, 20 April 1998 and No. 4, 27 April 1998.

19. Copeland (1993) comes to the same conclusion. This bargain is not only limited to the politics of enlargement. In the EU's general external relations, a reference to the need for co-operation with the aim of preventing illegal immigration can already be found in several agreements with third countries. As of February 1996, such a clause figured in the agreements with the Baltic states, Slovenia, Armenia, Azerbaijan, Belarus, Georgia, Kazakhstan, Kyrgyzstan and Russia. In the agreements with Egypt, Jordan, Lebanon, Morocco and Tunisia, a dialogue on problems related to illegal immigration is foreseen as a part of the social dialogue. In addition, these agreements foresee co-operation facilitating the resettlement of individuals who are to be repatriated as a consequence of their illegal status. In the light of the Justice and Home Affairs Council's decision of 23 November 1995 on incorporating readmission clauses in mixed agreements between the EU and its member states with third countries, it is to be expected that such clauses will appear in many such future agreements. Answers of the European Commission of 13 February 1996 to the questions raised by MEP, Philippe de Coene (H-0116/96).

20. *Uniting Europe* No. 13, 29 June 1998.

5 A Clash of Regimes? European versus International Refugee Protection

By co-operating in asylum and immigration matters, EU member states have developed a new set of institutions and norms for handling asylum claims which redefine the traditional approach of the international refugee regime and establish a distinct regional system of international co-operation amongst European countries referred to here as the European refugee regime. This co-operation, once limited to EU member states, has now transcended the Union's borders and led to the gradual incorporation of Central and Eastern Europe. In this final chapter the Europeanisation of refugee policies is interpreted in respect of its relationship with the international refugee regime and its impact on international relations. In doing so, it returns to the widening gap cited in Chapter 1 between an ever more complex problem structure on the one hand and stagnating policy responses on the other. This widening gap poses two major problems for the international community: the need to find a common definition of who qualifies as a refugee deserving international protection, and the difficulty of establishing a common basis for the allocation of states' responsibility for the protection of such refugees.

THE PRINCIPLE OF INTERNAL SECURITY

The analysis of the emergence of the European refugee regime amongst EU member states has shown that their co-operation was inspired less by a desire to enhance the system of international refugee protection in a common, harmonised approach than it was a reaction to the introduction of the free movement of persons in the context of European integration. Motivated by a perceived loss of control over the entry of third-country nationals, including asylum seekers, after the abolition of internal border controls, the driving principle for this co-operation has been framed as the safeguarding of internal security in the European Union and the member states. In the emergent European regime, these perceived losses of sovereignty were compensated by a re-enforcement of the external borders, the adoption of strict entry conditions for third-country nationals, and measures to counter bogus asylum claims. In this perspective, the claims of the individual refugee in need of protection are secondary to the primary objective of reducing immigration. Indeed, EU co-operation in refugee matters occupies only a small place in a much broader context of co-operation to enforce external borders and stem illegal immigration. The dominance of this context is reflected not only in the 'acquis' adopted in the fields of justice and home affairs, but also in the critical role played by these concerns in the member states' and the EU's relations with Central and Eastern Europe.

With this shift of perspective, the European refugee regime redefines the fundamental ideas and principles guiding international co-operation in refugee matters. Its leading motive is no longer the liberal ideal of providing protection for individuals, but rather the realist concern of the nation states with preserving sovereign control over the entry of aliens. As a consequence, this conceptual basis of the European refugee regime blurs the distinction between genuine refugees in need of international protection and voluntary migrants.

The notion of internal security has both a national and a European dimension. At the national level, the claims for restrictive asylum reforms and internal security are linked through a fear of welfare losses and a spread of racism and xenophobia. Within the European Union, the need to co-operate in asylum matters has been presented from the outset as a necessary compensation for the abolition of internal border controls in the single market with its associated 'dangers' for internal security. As a consequence, the issue of refugees was placed on the European agenda together with other perceived threats resulting from the lifting of internal borders, such as international crime, terrorism and drug trafficking. Accordingly, both the Schengen Agreement and the framework of co-operation under the third pillar of the Maastricht Treaty were composed of a range of disparate issues such as bogus asylum applications, the fight against illegal immigration and drug trafficking, and co-operation in police and judicial matters. The Amsterdam Treaty of 1997 loosened this institutional linkage of asylum and immigration matters with various forms of illegal activity by transferring the former from the third to the first pillar of the EC. Considering the aversion of most member states to any deepening of co-operation in these policy fields, it is unlikely that this will–at least in the short run–signify a re-orientation away from the primacy of control and internal security. To date, the purpose of the common asylum and immigration policies has not been to harmonise substantive asylum law and domestic status determination procedures, nor to combat inherent problems such as the phenomenon of 'refugees in orbit' or to settle the questionable legal status of *de facto* refugees. Their real goal has been to prevent abusive asylum claims, the enforcement of external borders, the restriction of entry conditions, the limitation of access to national asylum procedures through the application of the 'safe country' principles and the introduction of a system of redistribution to handle asylum claims which stipulates the exclusive responsibility of the first state entered by the asylum seeker. In sharp contrast to the global principles of the international refugee regime based on human rights, international soli-

darity and responsibility-sharing, this regional regime is dominated by the individual concerns of the sovereign nation states
to control and limit their exposure to refugee flows.

While in Western Europe, the impact of these new principles
has to some degree been compensated by a long liberal tradition in the protection of refugees and the rule of law, they are
likely to have much stronger consequences in the newly liberalised countries of Central and Eastern Europe. The analysis of
the various bilateral and multilateral attempts by Western European countries to export their refugee policies demonstrates the
dominance of national interests and the fear of losing control
over immigration from the poorer parts of the world. Both national policies and co-operative initiatives of the EU member
states *vis-à-vis* the CEECs originally focused exclusively on the
strengthening of the Eastern borders and the fight against illegal immigration, whilst ignoring the absence of a comparable
humanitarian tradition in the former Communist countries and
their lack of experience in refugee matters. Accordingly, the
subsequent support for the accession of these countries to the
fundamental treaties of the international refugee regime was
inspired less by the ideals of international solidarity than by the
national interest in including these (future) 'safe third countries'
in the system of redistribution established in the EU.

This tension between the protectionist principles of the extending European regime on the one hand and the liberal values of international law on the other lies at the heart of the
CEECs' contemporary efforts to implement the EU 'acquis' in
asylum and immigration matters. It is expressed both at the
level of actors contributing to the establishment of asylum and
immigration policies in the CEECs and in the legislative adaptation processes in these countries. Chapter 3 describes the
competition between the 'advocates' of the rights of refugees
and liberal values such as the UNHCR, NGOs or the Council of
Europe on the one hand and member states' bilateral and multilateral activities, in particular the 'Budapest Group' with its focus
on the fight against illegal immigration and the promotion of
strict border regimes, on the other. This competition is mirrored

in the legislative processes analysed in Chapter 4, which document a shift from an initially loose regulation of migratory regimes after the fall of Communism to the effort to reconcile basic humanitarian standards and the rule of law with the adoption of strict entry conditions and swift asylum procedures.

THE NORMS OF REDISTRIBUTION

Under the primacy of the principle of internal security, the norms constituting the European refugee regime have modified the traditional separation of general obligations at the international level and specific traditions and legislation at the national level. This clear separation of the more normative international and the more operative national levels is at the core of the traditional international regime, which is based on the individual responsibility of each nation state to fulfil its obligations under the international agreements. The fundamental norm in the international refugee regime, derived from the general commitment to universal human rights, is that of non-refoulement, which prohibits states from returning any person whose life or freedom would otherwise be threatened. As was pointed out in Chapter 1, this customary norm exceeds the more limited international right of asylum, which is basically a prerogative of individual states and represents the crucial limit to their sovereign power to decide on the entry and stay of foreigners on their territory. From this perspective, the normative provisions of the European refugee regime tend to weaken the individual state's commitment under the international refugee regime in so far as they establish a system of redistribution which diffuses responsibility and blurs accountability among the participating states.

This argument is underpinned by the central instruments of the European refugee regime, notably: the redistributive mechanism established amongst EU member states by the Schengen and the Dublin Agreements; the extension of this system to the countries of Central and Eastern Europe through the notion of 'safe third countries' and the conclusion of readmission agreements; and the concomitant efforts to regionalise the refugee problem and to prevent the arrival of large numbers of asylum seekers and refugees in Western Europe.

With regard to asylum seekers, the Schengen and the Dublin Agreements stipulate that it is the exclusive responsibility of one member state to examine an asylum claim. The basis for the allocation of such responsibility is the principle of first contact, in so far as the first state which allows an asylum seeker to enter the common territory, either *de facto* through the crossing of a border or legally, for instance by issuing a visa, is responsible. Accordingly, the other member states agree to respect the decision of the country responsible with regard to the result of the status determination procedure. This mutual recognition is based on the assumption of a common standard of refugee law and the compatibility of national status determination procedures. As has been shown, however, this assumption does not conform to reality. Instead, domestic asylum regulations in the member states vary considerably. Nevertheless, the way in which member states continued to co-operate under the third pillar of the Maastricht Treaty clearly showed the states' reluctance to substantive harmonisation of domestic asylum policies.

Western governments have praised the responsibility system for handling asylum claims established under the Schengen and Dublin Agreements for its ability to strengthen the international refugee regime by providing a clearer delineation of responsibility and accountability for the provision of protection. In reality, however, both the contents of the Conventions and subsequent agreements together with states' practices indicate instead a blurring of obligations under international and national law. This is clearly documented in the complementary restrictions on the entry of third-country nationals through the strengthening of border regimes, the adoption of stringent visa requirements, and the introduction of carrier sanctions which constitute the primary focus of co-operation in justice and home affairs. The ineffective implementation of the Schengen and Dublin Agreements and the frequent refusal to readmit a person on the basis of these agreements are also indicators of a lack of co-operation. Moreover, both Agreements contain a clause which directly undermines their system of responsibility allocation: that is, the possibility for member states to apply the 'safe third country' rule to non-EU countries. Harmonised in the 1992 London Resolution, the application of this rule actually takes precedence over the allocation of responsibility within the Union.

While this transfer of responsibility within the European Union is backed up by a common liberal tradition and the existence of national asylum regulations including an independent judiciary supervising their implementation, it has serious implications for Central and Eastern Europe. Unlike Western European countries, these states did not formerly participate in the international refugee regime. At the time of their incorporation into this system of redistribution, they did not have a national tradition in asylum matters and lacked the basic institutional and legal infrastructure necessary to examine asylum claims. Not only does this lead to a serious blurring of the questions of responsibility and accountability in refugee protection, but it may also be in breach of international law, for example through the refoulement of persons in need of protection to places where they may suffer serious human rights' violations. The proliferation of this system of redistribution further east and south may provoke a 'domino effect', where refugees and asylum seekers are progressively shifted back into regions where their fundamental human rights are not guaranteed.

The two central instruments leading to this extension of the European refugee regime are the notion of 'safe third countries' and the conclusion of readmission agreements. The notion of a 'safe country' is one of the key principles contained in the Schengen and Dublin Agreements and assumes the existence of basic human rights standards, including the observation of the norm of non-refoulement in that country. In its application to Central and Eastern Europe, however, this notion has been defined in a very broad fashion. The common Resolution on Safe Third Countries adopted in 1992 by the EU Ministers for

Immigration in London states two requirements for considering a country as safe–its adherence to the Geneva Refugee Convention, including the respect of the norm of non-refoulement, and the exclusion of torture and inhuman or degrading treatment. These, however, are only minimum requirements and do not guarantee the equivalence of domestic asylum procedures.

The predominance of a redistributive spirit over humanitarian norms is further documented in the instrument of readmission agreements which provide the legal basis for the application of the 'safe third country' rule. These agreements are a clear confirmation of the confusion of genuine refugees and illegal immigrants in the European refugee regime. They constitute a legal instrument for the effective rejection of undesired aliens to their countries of origin or to other third countries through which they have transited on their way to the European Union. This includes asylum seekers who are rejected without examination of their claim on the grounds of the 'safe third country' rule. According to the UNHCR, the application of these readmission agreements does not meet the humanitarian requirements of the international refugee regime and does not normally take account of the special situation of asylum seekers or guarantee access to a refugee status determination procedure.

In contrast to the Schengen and Dublin Agreements, these instruments are not designed for refugees and fail to stipulate the responsibility of the readmitting party to examine an asylum claim. When a person is readmitted on the basis of such an agreement, the authorities of the receiving countries do not normally receive formal notification of the fact that the person had previously applied for asylum in another country but that the asylum application was not examined on its merits. Consequently, the returnees may well have problems when submitting their application and may risk refoulement to a country where they are in danger of persecution. In short, the crude application of the 'safe third country' rule on the basis of readmission agreements not only diffuses the notion of responsibility, but also absolves the individual state from its human rights obligations under international law.

In addition to the redistributive system for handling asylum claims within the Union and with 'safe third countries', a third group of measures which constitute the European refugee regime are the totality of legal provisions governing the entry into the territory and accompanying policies for the prevention of refugee flows. With the Schengen Agreement, the major refugee receiving countries of the European Union have effectively exchanged the introduction of the free movement of persons inside the Union with the adoption of restrictive measures to strengthen its external borders. The development of the European refugee regime was accompanied by a significant intensification of control standards for non-EU members and the erection of additional barriers to immigration. Once again, these measures do not differentiate between refugees and voluntary migrants. As a general rule, third-country nationals can only enter the Union if they are in possession of a valid travel document, a valid visa where applicable, are not on the list of entry refusals, have justification for the purpose of stay or transit, and have sufficient means of subsistence. In accordance with these requirements, EU member states have engaged in a restrictive harmonisation of their visa policies. In order to enforce these tightened entry conditions, EU member states have agreed on the introduction of sanctions against transport agencies which enable the entry of persons not meeting these requirements. These tightened entry requirements establish a sort of pre-screening procedure outside the official administrative framework of refugee policy. With this pre-screening procedure, the first step in the determination of the well-foundedness of an asylum claim is transferred first to the embassy responsible for issuing or denying a visa, and then to the border police or transport agencies, neither of which are trained, competent or even accountable in these matters.

The dominance of the norms of redistribution is finally exemplified in the relatively new concept of temporary protection, which has entered the European refugee regime in the context of refugees from the former Yugoslavia. These *de facto* refugees form a particular group since they do not normally meet the criteria for refugee status as defined by the Geneva Convention but are nevertheless tolerated on a less formal basis. Although the EU member states have discussed the establishment of a system of 'burden-sharing' for the temporary protection of these refugees, the broader approach developed with regard to the crisis in the former Yugoslavia reveals the limits of these endeavours. Member states focused on preventing these refugees from entering their territories. To this end, two strategies were developed: the 'internalisation' of civil war victims in so-called 'safe havens' within their area of origin which are under the protection of the international organisations and NGOs; and the 'containment' of refugee flows within the broader area of the country of origin. Here too, the new policies re-define the traditional obligations of each nation state under the international refugee regime and tend to shift the responsibility for providing protection away from the domestic asylum determination procedures and towards new categories of actors, namely the UNHCR and NGOs within the regions of origin.

THE RULES OF INTERGOVERNMENTALISM

The third impact of the European refugee regime on the traditional system of international co-operation for the protection of refugees occurs at the level of the institutional rules which guide this co-operation. The European refugee regime redefines the traditional separation of general obligations at the international level under the auspices of a formally independent international organisation (the UNHCR) from their implementation in the nation states by introducing a new level of co-operation among member state executives, here referred to as intergovernmentalism. These intergovernmental rules represent a distinct form of governance which is neither national, European, nor international. While one could argue that international law in general is rarely the outcome of democratic deliberations but rather the product of consultations among national governments, in this policy field the features of intergovernmentalism are particularly important since they have evolved outside an already existing framework for international co-operation. Co-operation among EU member states has detached refugee policies from the traditional institutions of the international refugee regime, the United Nations with the UNHCR and, at the regional European level, the Council of Europe. Not only are traditional international actors excluded, but this co-operation also occurs outside the traditional domestic framework of political deliberation between different ministries and political parties and relatively independent of the supranational institutions of the European Union. This form of intergovernmentalism strengthens the role of particular members of the national executives, mainly within the Ministries of the Interior which, given their professional concern with questions of border control and internal security, play a determining role when it comes to establishing the primary goal of increasing state capacities to control and reduce (illegal) immigration.

In Chapter 2 the institutional features of the emergence of the European refugee regime are analysed in detail. It was shown that the structure of intergovernmental co-operation in asylum and immigration matters has its roots in informal forums outside the Community framework which operated screened from public scrutiny and free from democratic control. The promotion of co-operation among a limited number of traditional refugee receiving countries in the Schengen group, until the signature of the Second Schengen Agreement in 1990, played a crucial role in the adoption of common policies which were then transmitted to the more heterogeneous negotiations among all member states in the Ad Hoc Group Immigration and later under the third pillar of the Maastricht Treaty. With this polity of concentric circles, the traditional receiving countries acted as a motor for EU-wide co-operation, which allowed them to establish a system of negative redistribution for handling asylum claims within the Union. This system led, and still leads, to the progressive transformation of the Southern transit countries into receiving countries.

Despite the integration of this co-operation into the Community framework with the third pillar of the Maastricht Treaty, the intergovernmental forums have largely retained this mode of operation. Whereas the Schengen and the Dublin Agreements had to be ratified by the national parliaments, the formally non-binding resolutions and conclusions adopted after Maastricht are usually directly translated into national regulations by the competent minister. Neither the European Parliament nor national legislators have so far participated in drafting common 'European' policies. This democratic deficit is accentuated by the absence of judicial control over the intergovernmental agreements and activities under the third pillar. To date, neither the European Court of Justice nor the national courts have had jurisdictional power over these instruments. How far this inter-governmentalism will change with a transfer of the areas of asylum and immigration to the first pillar of the Union–as decided at the intergovernmental conference in Amsterdam in summer 1997–is unclear, but the refusal of member-state governments to introduce majority voting for these issues may well indicate that it will remain much as it is.

Apart from this formal level of policy-making, the rules of intergovernmentalism have an important impact on the implementation of the EU refugee regime and its extension to other countries. Within the European Union, the implementation of the common provisions of the Schengen Agreement or the instruments adopted under the third pillar tend to follow national interests. The most striking example of this is the fact that the original issue of this co-operation, the abolition of internal border controls and the introduction of free movement, is still not in place. Neither in the Schengen group, which originally wanted to pre-date the freedom of movement, nor in the Union have internal border controls been fully removed. Instead, the Amsterdam Treaty of 1997 postponed the introduction of free movement to an open date when the 'necessary compensation measures' are in place. Apart from the norm of free movement, the other provisions of the Schengen Agreement also appear to have been implemented in an inconsistent manner, with national governments tending to enforce those provisions which suit their interests while neglecting those that do not. An interesting finding is that, despite its flexible nature, intergovernmentalism can have a very serious impact on national policies. In two major refugee receiving countries, France and Germany, the implementation of the Schengen Agreement was said to require the restriction of the highly symbolic asylum right in the national constitutions.

The significance of the rules of intergovernmental co-operation is finally documented in the extension of the European refugee regime *vis-à-vis* Central and Eastern Europe. This extension was initiated by single member states in their drive to curb illegal immigration and reduce the numbers of asylum seekers through the designation of some CEECs as 'safe third countries' and the conclusion of readmission agreements. It was not originally part of the official relations between the EU and these associated countries: asylum and immigration issues did not figure in the legal 'acquis' of the Union which must be adopted in order to acquire membership in the first years of association. The introduction of these matters into the pre-accession strategy was an initiative by intergovernmental actors. Linking the extension of the emergent European refugee regime with the broader question of EU enlargement, the member states gathered legitimation for their interest in exporting their policies and could exert additional pressure on the associated countries to adopt them. Given the perseverance of intergovernmentalism in the framework of co-operation in the EU, member state executives now play an increasingly important role in the enlargement process and have contributed to the progressive expansion of membership conditions.

CONCLUSION

In the last two decades we have witnessed a significant shift in European policies towards migration in general and asylum seekers in particular, and which touch both the reorganisation of territorial border regimes in Western and Central-Eastern Europe and the gradual transformation of the international system of co-operation for the protection of refugees. This book has identified three major dynamics underlying these processes: the growing concern among Western European countries with the increasing numbers of asylum seekers and illegal immigrants; the dynamics of European integration and, in particular, the prospect of the free movement of persons; and the opening up of the Eastern bloc, perceived by the West as generating large incoming flows of economic migrants and asylum seekers into their territory. The historical coincidence of these three developments reinforced Western endeavours to restrict their asylum and immigration policies not only domestically and in the EU, but also through the export of restrictive policies to Central and Eastern Europe and the gradual incorporation of the newly liberalised countries into the emerging system of EU co-operation in these matters. Induced, at a purely intergovernmental level, through the unilateral and bilateral activities of single member states, the CEECs' adaptation to this regional refugee and immigration regime is now an integral part of the EU pre-accession strategy.

The effects of these changes are significant. The emergent pan-European refugee regime has considerable consequences for the traditional framework of international co-operation for the protection of refugees, in terms of guiding principles, operational norms and institutional rules. Taken together, this new system of international co-operation has shifted the issue of refugees away from its original human rights context and towards the sphere of internal security and control. Returning to the two fundamental challenges facing refugee protection today, these developments are indicative of a weakening of the international refugee regime. The principles, norms and rules of European co-operation aggravate the difficulty of distinguishing genuine refugees deserving international protection from other kinds of voluntary migrants and tend to diffuse the nation states' responsibilities under international law. While in Western Europe, these restrictive developments are attenuated by several decades of democracy and modern human rights practices, their impact on the asylum policies of the acceding Central and Eastern European countries is incisive. Having been unilaterally incorporated into the system of redistribution established amongst the EU countries, these states adopt restrictive policies without sharing the humanitarian tradition and without a set of historically rooted institutions to safeguard the notion of refugee protection. From an international law perspective, these processes are all the more worrying because of their inherently expanding dynamics. The rapid and uncontrolled proliferation of instruments such as the 'safe country rule' or readmission agreements with countries not party to the Geneva Convention—such as Belarus, Russia and Ukraine—may lead to the chain deportation of asylum seekers to places where their lives or basic freedoms are threatened. This would constitute a violation of the principle of non-refoulement and, as a consequence, be a serious offence against the spirit of the international refugee regime.

The only way to counteract these developments would be to reaffirm liberal values in the West and to foster these values to the newly liberalised countries of Central and Eastern Europe. Together with this normative reorientation comes the need to prevent a negative redistribution of the 'burden' of asylum seekers, refugees and illegal migrants from traditional refugee receiving countries to those which, given their geographical position, are first exposed to migratory flows. In particular, this concerns the restrictive application of the 'safe third country' rule and the indiscriminate use of readmission agreements. Finally, EU member states need to clarify their attitude to Eastern enlargement, in so far as a narrow concentration on restriction and control may indeed lead to the erection of new borders within Europe which, by impeding the free movement of persons, challenges the very idea of European unification. This challenge does not concern the EU's relations with Central and Eastern Europe alone, but raises the more fundamental question as to what kind of European Union we aspire to–and the place it reserves for the notion of human rights.

References

Adling, Thomas and Jahn, Werner (1997). 'Fluchtbewegungen aus Südost-europa', in S. Angenendt (ed.), *Migration und Flucht. Aufgaben und Strategien für Deutschland, Europa und die internationale Gemeinschaft.* Munich: Oldenbourg.

Amnesty International (1993). 'Open Letter to the Meeting of Immigration Ministers', 25 May.

Arboleda, Eduardo and Hoy, Ian (1993). 'The Convention Refugee Definition in the West: Disharmony of Interpretation and Application', *International Journal of Refugee Law* 5(1), 66–90.

Bigo, Didier (ed.) (1992). '*L'Europe des polices et de la sécurité intérieure'*. Brussels: Editions Complexe.

Bolten, J. J. (1991). 'From Schengen to Dublin: the New Frontiers of Refugee Law', in H. Meijers, J. J. Bolten and A. Cruz, *Schengen. Internationalisation of Central Chapters of the Law on Aliens, Refugees, Security and the Police.* Leiden: NJCM Boekerij.

Busch, Heiner (1996a). 'Die „Dritte Säule"? der Europäischen Union–Bilanz des institutionellen Rahmens der EU-Innenpolitik'. *Bürgerrechte und Polizei/CILIP* 53(1), 6–12.

Busch, Heiner (1996b). 'Polizeihilfe für die Polizeien in Mittel- und Osteuropa– Die Helfer helfen sich selbst', *Bürgerrechte und Polizei/CILIP* 55(3), 7–14.

CAHAR (Ad Hoc Committee of Experts on the Legal Aspects of Territorial Asylum, Refugees and Stateless Persons) (1997). 'Summary Description of Asylum Procedures in Selected Member states of the Council of Europe (Czech Republic, Lithuania, Poland, Romania, Slovakia and the Republic of Slovenia)'. Prepared by Wladislaw Czaplinski, CAHAR (97) 2.

Conseil de l'Europe (1996). *Activités du Conseil de l'Europe dans le domaine des migrations.* Strasbourg: Conseil de l'Europe.

Copeland, Emily (1993). 'East-West Migration in the Post-Cold War Period: Its Impact on States' Strategies and International Institutions', in M-B. Rocha-Trindade, (ed.) *Migration Trends in Europe. Europe's New Architecture.* Lisbon: Universidade Aberta.

Council of Europe (1991a). 'Opening Address by Catherine Lalumiere, Secretary General of the Council of Europe at the Conference of Ministers on the

Movement of Persons Coming from Central and Eastern European Countries', Vienna, 24 January 1991, Document 25 (91).

Council of Europe (1991b). 'Communiqué. Ministerial Conference on the
Movement of Persons from Central and Eastern European Countries'. Vienna, 24–25 January, Document MMP (91).

Council of Europe (1996). 'Final Communiqué. Sixth Conference of the European Ministers Responsible for Immigration', Warsaw, 16–18 June 1996,
Document MMG, 6 (96) 5 final.

Council of the European Union General Secretariat (1994) 'Berlin Declaration
on Increased Co-operation in Combating Drug Crime and Organized Crime
in Europe', Berlin, 8 September 1994, press release 9345/94 (Presse 182),
14 August 1994.

Cruz, Antonio (1993). 'Schengen, Ad Hoc Immigration Group and other Intergovernmental Bodies', Briefing Paper of the Churches Committee for Migrants in Europe No. 12, Brussels.

Cullen, David (1995). 'Variable Geometry and Overlapping Circles', in R. Bieber
and J. Monar (eds.), Justice and Home Affairs in the European Union. The
Development of the Third Pillar. Brussels: European Interuniversity Press.

Czaplinski, Wladyslaw (1994). 'Aliens and Refugee Law in Poland: Recent
Developments', International Journal of Refugee Law 6(4), 636–42.

Danish Refugee Council (1998). Safe Third Country Policy in European
Countries. Internet: http://www.drc.dk.

Dietrich, Helmut (1998). 'Deusch-polnische Polizeikooperation. Flüchtling-
spolitik als Schrittmacher', Bürgerrechte und Polizei/CILIP 59(1), 4–15.

Drüke, Luise (1993). 'Refugee Protection in the Post-Cold War Europe: Asylum in the Schengen and EC Harmonization Process', in A. Pauly (ed.),
Les accords de Schengen: abolition des frontières intérieures ou menace
pour les libertés publiques. Maastricht: European Institute of Public Administration.

EC Commission (1997a). Factual Document on Asylum. Working Document
in Preparation of the Ministerial Meeting between the EU and the CEECs
on 27.5.1997 within the Context of the Structured Dialogue. Brussels: EC
Commission.

EC Commission (1997b). Agenda 2000: for a Stronger and Wider Union.
Brussels: EC Commission.

ECRE (1993). Asylum in Europe. London: European Council on Refugees
and Exiles.

ECRE (1995). Note on the Harmonization of the Interpretation of Article 1 of
the 1951 Geneva Convention. London: European Council on Refugees
and Exiles.

ECRE and Amnesty International (1995). 'ECRE and Amnesty International
Believe that Minimum Guarantees for Asylum Procedures Are Insufficient',
press release, 10 March 1995.

Engelbrekt, Kjell (1994). 'Bulgaria and the Problem of Immigration', *RFE/RL Research Report* 3(25), 37–40.

EP (1987). *Report Drawn up on Behalf of the Committee on Legal Affairs and Citizens' Rights on the Right of Asylum.* Rapporteur: H. O. Vetter, Document A2-227/86, Brussels, 23 February 1987.

EP (1995). *Report on the Draft Council Recommendation concerning a Specimen Bilateral Readmission Agreement, Committee of Fundamental Freedoms and Internal Affairs.* Rapporteur: Claudia Roth. Document A4-0184/95, Brussels.

EP (1997). Directorate General for Research 'Working Paper on Migration and Asylum in Central and Eastern Europe, Meeting of the Committee of Civil Liberties and Internal Affairs with the corresponding committees in Brussels, 10–11 June 1996', *People's Europe Series* W-9 EN-2-97.

Fisher, Sharon (1994). 'Immigrants and Refugees in Slovakia', *RFE/RL Research Report* 3(24), 42–44.

Fortescue, John Adrian (1995). 'First Experiences with the Implementation of the Third Pillar Provisions', in R. Bieber and J. Monar (eds.), *Justice and Home Affairs in the European Union. The Development of the Third Pillar.* Brussels: European Interuniversity Press.

Fortin, Antonio (1993). *The 'Safe Third Country' Policy in the Light of the International Obligations of Countries vis-à-vis Refugees and Asylum Seekers.* London: UNHCR.

Fullerton, Mary-Ellen (1996). 'Hungary, Refugees, and the Law of Return', *International Journal of Refugee Law* 8(4), 499–531.

German Ministry of the Interior (1996). *Schengen-Erfahrungsbericht.* Bonn: Ministry of the Interior.

Glahn, Wiltrud von (1992). *Der Kompetenzwandel internationaler Flüchtlingsorganisationen–vom Völkerbund bis zu den Vereinten Nationen.* Baden-Baden: Nomos.

Goodwin-Gill, Gil (1995). 'Asylum: Law and the Politics of Change', *International Journal of Refugee Law* 7(1), 1–18.

Grabbe, Heather (1998). 'A Partnership for Accession? The Nature, Scope and Implications of EU Conditionality on CEE Applicants for Membership'. Florence: manuscript.

Grabbe, Heather and Hughes, Kirsty (1998). *Enlarging the EU Eastwards.* London: Royal Institute of International Affairs.

Grahl-Madsen (1980). *Territorial Asylum.* New York: Oceana.

Hailbronner, Kay (1989). *Möglichkeiten und Grenzen einer europäischen Koordinierung des Einreise- und Asylrechts: Ihre Auswirkungen auf das Asylrecht der Bundesrepublik Deutschland.* Baden-Baden: Nomos.

Hailbronner, Kay (1993). *Die Rechtsstellung der De Facto-Flüchtlinge in den EG-Staaten: Rechtsvergleichung und Europäische Harmonisierung.* Baden-Baden: Nomos.

Hailbronner, Kay (1995). 'Die Europäische Asylrechtsharmonisierung nach dem Vertrag von Maastricht', *Zeitschrift für Ausländerrecht und Ausländerpolitik* 19(1), 3–13.

Hailbronner, Kay (1996). *Rückübernahme eigener und fremder Staatsangehöriger. Völkerrechtliche Verpflichtungen der Staaten*. Heidelberg: Universitätsverlag.

Hathaway, James (1984). 'The Evolution of Refugee Status in International Law: 1920–1950', *The International and Comparative Law Quarterly* 33, 348–80.

Hathaway, James (1991). 'Reconceiving Refugee Law as Human Rights Law', *Journal of Refugee Studies* 4(122), 109–34.

Heinelt, Hubert (ed.) (1994). *Zuwanderungspolitik in Europa. Nationale Politiken–Gemeinsamkeiten und Unterschiede*. Opladen: Leske und Budrich.

Hix, Simon and Niessen, Jan (1996). 'Reconsidering European Migration Policies. The 1996 Intergovernmental Conference and the Reform of the Maastricht Treaty'. Briefing Paper of the Migration Policy Group. Brussels: the Churches Commission for Migrants in Europe.

Holborn, Louise (1975). *Refugees, a Problem of Our Time: The Work of the United Nations High Commissioner for Refugees*. Metuchen, N.J.

Hoskova, Mahulena (1996). 'Das neue slowakische Asylrecht', *Zeitschrift für Ausländerrecht und Ausländerpolitik* 3(2), 129–33.

Intergovernmental Consultations on Asylum and Migration Policy in Europe, North America, and Australia (1995). *Summary Descriptions of Asylum Procedures in Europe, North America and Australia*. Geneva: Intergovernmental Consultations.

Intergovernmental Consultations on Asylum and Migration Policy in Europe, North America, and Australia (1997). *Inventory of Readmission Agreements*. Geneva: Intergovernmental Consultations.

Joly, Danièle (1996). *Haven or Hell? Asylum Policies and Refugees in Europe*. London and New York: Macmillan.

Kimminich, Otto (1978). 'Die Geschichte des Asylrechts', in Amnesty International (ed.), *Bewährungsprobe für ein Grundrecht: Art. 16 Abs.2 Satz 2 Grundgesetz: Politisch Verfolgte genießen Asylrecht*. Baden-Baden: Nomos.

Krasner, Stephen (1982). 'Structural Causes and Regime Consequences: Regimes as Intervening Variables', in S. Krasner (ed.), *International Regimes*. Ithaca and London: Cornell University Press.

Lavenex, Sandra (1998a). 'Transgressing Borders: The Emergent European Refugee Regime and "Safe Third Countries"', in A. Cafruny and P. Peters (eds.), *The Union and the World*. The Hague: Kluwer Law International.

Lavenex, Sandra (1998b). 'Asylum, Immigration and Central-Eastern Europe: Challenges to EU Enlargement', *European Foreign Affairs Review* 3(2), 275–94.

Lavenex, Sandra (forthcoming). 'The Europeanisation of Refugee Policy: between Human Rights and Internal Security', Ph.D thesis, Florence: European University Institute.

Lee, Luke T. (1986). 'Towards a World without Refugees: the United Nations Group of Governmental Experts on International Co-operation to Avert New Flows of Refugees', *The British Yearbook of International Law* 6(2), 317–36.

Leuthardt, Beat (1997). *Europas neuer Pförtner. Litauen im Schatten des deutschen Asylrechts.* Bonn: von Loeper.

Lobkowicz, Wenceslas de (1990). 'Quelle libre circulation des personnes en 1993?', *Revue du marché commun* 334, 93–102.

Lobkowicz, Wenceslas de (1993a). 'L'Union Européenne et le Droit d'Asile'. Paper presented at the workshop "Evolutions récentes du droit des réfugiés en Europe" at the Collège d'Europe in Bruges, 25 March.

Lobkowicz, Wenceslas de (1993b). 'La coopération intergouvernementale dans le domaine des migrations: de l'Acte Unique à Maastricht'. Paper presented at the Collège d'Europe in Bruges, 9 September .

Loescher, Gil (1989). 'The European Community and Refugees', *International Affairs* 65(1), 617–36.

Loescher, Gil (1996). *Beyond Charity: International Co-operation and the Global Refugee Crisis.* New York and Oxford: Oxford University Press.

Mahmood, Shiraz (1995). 'The Schengen Information System: An Inequitable Data Protection Regime', *International Journal of Refugee Law* 7(2), 179–200.

Melander, Göran (1978). *Refugees in Orbit.* Oxford: Oxford University Press.

Münch, Ursula (1992). *Asylpolitik in der Bundesrepublik Deutschland. Entwicklungen und Alternativen.* Opladen: Leske und Budrich.

Myers, Philip (1995). 'European Police Co-operation under Title VI TEU–A Balance Sheet After the Cannes European Council', in R. Bieber and J. Monar (eds.), *Justice and Home Affairs in the European Union. The Development of the Third Pillar.* Brussels: European Interuniversity Press.

Nanz, Klaus-Peter (1994). 'Das Schengener Übereinkommen: Personenfreizügigkeit in integrationspolitischer Perspektive', *Integration* 17(2), 92–108.

Noiriel, Gérard (1991). *La Tyrannie du National. Le droit d'asile en Europe 1793–1993.* Paris: Calmann-Levy.

O'Keefe, David (1996). 'A Critical View of the Third Pillar', in A. Pauly (ed.), *De Schengen à Maastricht: voie royale et course d'obstacles.* Maastricht: European Institute of Public Administration.

Pataki, Judith (1994). 'The Recent History of the Hungarian Refugee Problem', *RFE/RL Research Report* 3(24), 34–38.

Pauly, Alexis (ed.) (1993). *Les accords de Schengen: Abolition des frontières intérieures ou menace pour les libertés publiques.* Maastricht: European Institute of Public Administration.

Pehe, Jiri (1994). 'Immigrants in the Czech Republic', *RFE/RL Research Report* 3(24), 30–33.

Plender, Richard (1995). 'Asylum Policy: Deficits of Intergovernmental Co-operation', in R. Bieber and J. Monar (eds.), *Justice and Home Affairs in the European Union. The Development of the Third Pillar.* Brussels: European Interuniversity Press.

Polish Government, Committee for European Integration (1997). *National Strategy for Integration.* Warsaw, January .

Rijt, Wouter van de (1997). 'Schengen depuis le 26 mars 1995', in M. den Boer (ed.), *The Implementation of Schengen: First the Widening, Now the Deepening.* Maastricht: European Institute of Public Administration.

Rupprecht, Reinhard and Hellenthal, Markus (eds.) (1992). *Innere Sicherheit im Europäischen Binnenmarkt.* Gütersloh: Bertelsmann.

Salomon, Kim (1991). *Refugees in the Cold War.* Lund: Lund University Press.

Santel, Bernhard (1995). 'Loss of Control: the Build-up of a European Migration and Asylum Regime', in R. Miles and D. Thränhardt (eds.), *Migration and European Integration: the Dynamics of Inclusion and Exclusion.* London: Pinter.

Schatzer, Peter (1995). 'Dealing with Migration Pressures affecting Central and Eastern Europe', in S. Perrakis (ed.), *Immigration and European Union: Building on a Comprehensive Approach.* Athens: Sakkoulas.

Schieffer, Martin (1997). 'The Readmission of Third-Country Nationals within Bilateral and Multilateral Frameworks', in M. den Boer (ed.), *The Implementation of Schengen: First the Widening, Now the Deepening.* Maastricht: European Institute of Public Administration.

Sedlemeier, Ulrich (1994). *The European Union's Association Policy towards Central and Eastern Europe: Political and Economic Rationalities in Conflict.* Brighton: Sussex European Institute.

Sedelmeier, Ulrich and Wallace, Helen (1996). 'Policies towards Central and Eastern Europe', in H. Wallace and W. Wallace (eds.), *Policy-making in the European Union,* Oxford: Oxford University Press.

Shafir, Michael (1994). 'Immigrants in Romania', *RFE/RL Research Reports* 3(25), 41–46.

Sjøberg, Tommie (1991). *The Powers and the Persecuted: the Refugee Problem and the Intergovernmental Committee on Refugees (IGCR) 1938–1947.* Lund: Lund University Press.

Spijkerboer, Thomas (1993). *A Bird's Eye View of Asylum Law in Eight European Countries.* Amsterdam: ACM.

Stainsby, R. A. (1990). 'Asylum Seekers in Poland: The Catalyst for a New Refugee and Asylum Policy in Europe', *International Journal of Refugee Law* 2(4), 636–41.

Standing Committee of Experts in International Immigration, Refugee and Criminal Law (eds.) (1993). 'Commentary on the Draft Conclusions of the European Ministers Responsible for Immigration Affairs Meeting in London on 30 November 1992 and the Not Yet Adopted Resolution concerning Family Reunification'. Utrecht: Dutch Centre for Immigrants.

Standing Committee of Experts in International Immigration, Refugee and Criminal Law (1994). *Who is a 'Refugee'?*. Utrecht: Dutch Centre for Immigrants, June.

Steiner, Erich and Sladewski, Daniel (1995). 'Polen', in Basso-Sekretariat Berlin (ed.), *Festung Europa auf der Anklagebank. Dokumentation des Basso-Tribunals zum Asylrecht in Europa*. Munster: Westfählisches Dampfboot.

Suhrke, Astri (1993). 'A Crisis Diminished: Refugees in the Developing World', *International Journal* 48(2), 215–39.

Teitgen-Colly, Catherine (1994). 'Le droit d'asile: la fin des illusions', *Actualité Juridique–droit administratif*, 97–114.

Thorburn, Joanne (1995). 'Transcending Boundaries: Temporary Protection and Burden-sharing in Europe', *International Journal of Refugee Law* 7(3), 459–80.

UNHCR (1992). *Background Information on the Situation of Slovenia in the Context of the Safe Third Country Concept*. Geneva: UNHCR.

UNHCR (1995a). *The State of Refugees in the World*. Geneva: UNHCR.

UNHCR (1995b). *Update: UNHCR concerned by EU Agreement on Asylum Procedures*. Brussels: UNHCR.

UNHCR (1995c). *Notes on Agents of Persecution*. Brussels: UNHCR.

UNHCR (1995d). *Background Information on the Situation of Non-Europeans in Hungary*. Geneva: UNHCR.

UNHCR (1996a). *Summary of UNHCR Activities in Central Europe*. Geneva: UNHCR.

UNHCR (1996b). *Analysis of Gaps in Central European Asylum Systems*. Geneva: UNHCR.

UNHCR (1997). *Background Information on the Asylum System in Romania*. Geneva: UNHCR.

Warning, Georg (1991). 'Das neue Asylrecht in der Tschechoslowakei', *Monatshefte für Osteuropäisches Recht* 33, 23–32.

Weber, Steven (1995). 'European Union Conditionality', in B. Eichengreen, J. Frieden and J. von Hagen (eds.), *Politics and Institutions in an Integrated Europe*. Berlin: Springer.

Weil, Patrick (1991). *La France et ses étrangers: L'aventure d'une politique de l'immigration 1938–1991*. Paris: Calmann-Levy.

Weydenthal, Jan B. de (1994). 'Immigration into Poland', *RFE/RL Research Report* 2(24), 39–41.

Wolken, Simone (1998a). *Das Grundrecht auf Asyl als Gegenstand der Innen- und Rechtspolitik der Bundesrepublik Deutschland*. Frankfurt a.M.: Lang.

Wolken, Simone (1988b). 'Antikommunismus und Eurozentrismus als Einflußfaktoren Bundesdeutscher Asylpolitik', in A. Ashkenasi (ed.), *Das Weltweite Flüchtlingsproblem. Sozialwissenschaftliche Versuche der Annäherung.* Bremen: Bertelsmann.

Zarjevski, Yéfime (1988). *A Future Preserved. International Assistance to Refugees.* Oxford: Oxford University Press.

Zolberg, Aristide, Surhke, Astri and Aguayo, Sergio (1989). *Escaping from Violence: Conflict and Refugee Crisis in the Developing World.* New York: Oxford University Press.

Index

New

from

CENTRAL EUROPEAN UNIVERSITY PRESS

LANGUAGE: A RIGHT AND A RESOURCE
Approaches to Linguistic Human Rights

Edited by

Miklós Kontra (Hungarian Academy of Sciences)
Robert Phillipson (Roskilde University, Denmark)
Tove Skutnabb-Kangas (Roskilde University, Denmark)
Tibor Várady (Central European University, Budapest)

Linguistic Human Rights (LHR) is a fast growing new area of study combining the principles of national and international law with the study of language as a central dimension of ethnicity. Implementation of these principles is aimed at ensuring that no state or society violates these basic rights.

This path-breaking study broadens our knowledge of the important role of language in minority rights and in social and political struggles for LHRs. Exploring the interactions of linguistic diversity, biodiversity, the free market and human rights, the contributors present case studies to highlight such issues as Kurdish satellite TV attempting to create a virtual state on the air through trying to achieve basic LHR's for Kurds in Turkey; the implementation of LHRs in the Baltic states; and the obstacles met in education by Roma and the deaf in Hungary because of lack of appropriate LHRs.

Language: a Right and a Resource is a valuable multi-disciplinary text to be used in different areas of study in the legal profession, linguistics, cultural and political studies.

Contents

Chapter 1: Conceptualizing & implementing LHRs **GENERAL ISSUES Chapter 2:** International languages and international human rights **Chapter 3:** Heroes, rebels, communities and states in language rights activism and litigation **Chapter 4:** "Don't speak Hungarian in public!" **Chapter 5:** Common language problem **LEGAL ISSUES Chapter 6:** Existing rights of minorities and international law **Chapter 7:** Slovak state language law **MARKET ISSUES Chapter 8:** Market forces, language spread and linguistic diversity **Chapter 9:** Linguistic diversity, human rights and the free market **Chapter 10:** Language rights in the emerging world linguistic order **Chapter 11:** Separating language from ethnicity **Chapter 12:** Language policy in a changing society **EDUCATION & ETHNICITY ISSUES Chapter 13:** Recognition of sign language **Chapter 14:** LHRs problems among Romani and Boyash speakers of Hungary **Chapter 15:** Contempt for LHR in the service of the Catholic Church

October 1999
400 pages   (299 × 155mm)
Cloth ISBN: 963-9116-63-7 $49.95 / £31.95
Paperback ISBN: 963-9116-64-5 $23.95 / £14.95

Available at ALL good bookshops
Alternatively, order direct from:
US: Books International, PO Box 605, Herndon, VA 20172 Tel: +1 703 661 1500
UK / Europe: Plymbridge Distributors Ltd., Estover Road, Plymouth Tel: +44 1752 202 301
Other Regions: CEUP, Október 6. u. 12, 1051 Budapest, Hungary
Tel: +36 1 327 3181 Fax: +36 1 327 3183